# New York's Coldest Cases

# New York's Coldest Cases
*Ten Unsolved Murders That Rocked the Empire State*

David Bushman

and

Mark T. Givens

*Essex, Connecticut*

# Globe Pequot

An imprint of The Globe Pequot Publishing Group, Inc.
64 South Main Street
Essex, CT 06426
www.globepequot.com

Copyright © 2026 by David Bushman and Mark T. Givens

*All rights reserved.* No part of this book may be reproduced in any form or by any electronic or mechanical means, including information storage and retrieval systems, without written permission from the publisher, except by a reviewer who may quote passages in a review.

British Library Cataloguing in Publication Information available

**Library of Congress Cataloging-in-Publication Data**
Names: Bushman, David, 1955– author | Givens, Mark T. author
Title: New York's coldest cases : ten unsolved murders that rocked the
  Empire State / David Bushman and Mark T. Givens.
Description: Essex, Connecticut : Globe Pequot, [2026] | Includes
  bibliographical references. | Summary: "Ten of New York's most
  interesting murder mysteries are unraveled through the history of the
  victims, the suspects, and personal anecdotes of family and friends who
  were impacted by the deaths. The breakdown of the crime scene, timelines
  of the victims and the suspects, and the various clues give readers a
  personal guide to the unsolved murders that rocked New York"— Provided
  by publisher.
Identifiers: LCCN 2025038078 (print) | LCCN 2025038079 (ebook) | ISBN
  9781493091560 paperback | ISBN 9781493091577 epub
Subjects: LCSH: Murder—New York (State)—New York—Case studies | Cold
  cases (Criminal investigation)—New York (State)—New York
Classification: LCC HV6534.N5 B87 2026 (print) | LCC HV6534.N5 (ebook)
LC record available at https://lccn.loc.gov/2025038078
LC ebook record available at https://lccn.loc.gov/2025038079

# Contents

Introduction . . . . . . . . . . . . . . . . . . . . . . . . . . . . . .vii
CHAPTER 1: Who Wants to Kill a Millionaire? . . . . . . . . . . . . . . . 1
CHAPTER 2: The New York Ripper . . . . . . . . . . . . . . . . . . . . 15
CHAPTER 3: Who Is Buried in Greenfield Cemetery? . . . . . . . . . . . 37
CHAPTER 4: A Lady Vanishes . . . . . . . . . . . . . . . . . . . . . . . 49
CHAPTER 5: Farmhouse Tragedy . . . . . . . . . . . . . . . . . . . . . 65
CHAPTER 6: A Bridge Too Far . . . . . . . . . . . . . . . . . . . . . . 79
CHAPTER 7: The Sailor, the Baker, the Westchester Head Shaker . . . . . 103
CHAPTER 8: Locked and Loaded . . . . . . . . . . . . . . . . . . . . .125
CHAPTER 9: Who Ordered the Cement Shoes? . . . . . . . . . . . . . .135
CHAPTER 10: The Bomb Heard 'Round the World's Fair . . . . . . . . .151
Acknowledgments . . . . . . . . . . . . . . . . . . . . . . . . . . . .163
Bibliography . . . . . . . . . . . . . . . . . . . . . . . . . . . . . . .165
About the Authors . . . . . . . . . . . . . . . . . . . . . . . . . . . .175

# Introduction

"Cold cases are hot" may be a clichéd way to introduce this book, but it's true. An internet search for "best cold case podcasts" yields 549 hits, with titles ranging from *The Cold-Case Christianity Podcast* to *Lesbian Detectives* to *Otzi The Iceman Must Die*. Television, of course, loves cold cases, both fictional and real—*Cold Case, Cold Case Spotlight, Unsolved Mysteries, Cold Case Files, Cold Justice, Who Killed JonBenét Ramsey?*, yada yada. And books? Let's not even go there.

Estimates of the number of murders that go unsolved in the United States annually range between 30 and 50 percent—and that doesn't even account for wrongful convictions. According to FBI data, 346,000 cases of homicide and nonnegligent manslaughter went unsolved from 1965 to 2023. Any way you slice it, a lot of the people who commit murder walk away scot-free.

New York, according to the FBI, recorded about 80,000 homicides over that forty-eight-year span, second only to Texas. New York's clearance rate was 65 percent, meaning some 28,000 murders have gone unsolved. Not great, but a lot better than California's staggering total of 52,480.

The most famous cold case of all time? Almost certainly the Jack the Ripper murders in Whitehall, London, between 1888 and 1891 (canonically at least). Some of the many, many, *many* people obsessed with the Ripper maintain that he crossed the pond, landing in America in 1891, and may even have picked up right where he left off with the evisceration of Carrie Brown, a mysterious old drunkard known around Manhattan's East River waterfront bars for reciting entire passages of William Shakespeare in exchange for a few swigs from the bottle. The death of Brown, nicknamed Old Shakespeare, is the second oldest covered in these pages, after the 1870 slaying of wealthy financier Benjamin Nathan, proof that the Angel of Death is impervious to economic bias.

Because so many mobsters have called New York home, and because underworld etiquette requires that they clam up when asked—even on their deathbed—to identify their assassins, the state has been the setting for a formidable number of unsolved gangland killings. The thug we single out here is Abraham "Bo" Weinberg, a Dutch Schultz gunman who is himself a popular suspect in the unsolved murders of Jack "Legs" Diamond and Arnold Rothstein. On the other side of the law, NYPD officers Joseph Lynch and Ferdinand Socha perished while attempting to defuse a bomb at the 1940 World's Fair in Queens; the ensuing investigation turned up almost nothing of value but did lead to suspicion that our good chums the Brits may have been involved, under the direction of the "Man Called Intrepid" himself, Sir William Stephenson, the template for Ian Fleming's James Bond.

A family of farmers in upstate New York; a world-renowned bridge player/Lothario; a quiet, unassuming New York City laundryman; a ne'er-do-well Massachusetts Navy vet who had the misfortune of crossing paths one fateful day with the scion of the baking empire that has blessed us with Hostess cupcakes and Twinkies; a failed New York City writer who seemed to have vanished off the face of the earth; and a mystery woman whose very identity has baffled authorities for decades—in life they would seem to have had little in common, but in death they share an unfortunate distinction: all laid six feet under by murderers never held accountable for their sins. Here in these pages we remember them . . . and maybe even solve one or two of their murders.

I

# Who Wants to Kill a Millionaire?

*New York City*

Benjamin Nathan was probably exhausted when he finally went to bed the night of Thursday, July 28, 1870. A terrible storm had been building through the evening, bringing with it torrents of rain against a backdrop of lightning flashes. Earlier in the day, Nathan, a wealthy, semiretired financier, had traveled back to his stately brownstone mansion at 12 East 23rd Street, at the corner of Fifth Avenue, in Manhattan, leaving his wife and family back in their country estate in Morristown, New Jersey. Nathan had returned home on the eve of the anniversary of his mother's death, intending to honor her passing at his synagogue in the morning. After attending to some business that afternoon in his downtown offices, he came back home, later spending the evening visiting relatives, returning home a little before 10:00 p.m. Shortly after that, his son Frederick came home and stopped by Benjamin's bedroom to wish him goodnight. Benjamin asked if Frederick's younger brother, Washington, was home yet, and Frederick responded he didn't think so; by the time Washington did get home, around 12:15 a.m., his father was asleep, and the sprawling upscale estate was quiet.

Washington woke shortly before 6:00 a.m. the next morning, little prepared for the horrific sight he was about to discover. The house was still quiet as he put on his socks and, before changing out of his nightshirt, went downstairs intending to get a glass of ice water and to see if his father was awake yet. On his way, he ran into his brother Frederick, now stirring—Frederick said he needn't bother checking on their father, as he would certainly be up and about already. As he came down from the third floor to the second, where his father was staying, Washington suspected his brother was wrong, as the door to his father's bedroom was still firmly shut. Upon entering the room, he did not find his father oversleeping; the bed was unoccupied. However, looking in the direction of the adjoining room, which served as an office for his father, he saw the shape of a body lying face down in the doorway.

Washington apprehensively approached the body with mounting dread, not noticing that his stockinged feet were soaking up the blood that had saturated the carpet. The body appeared lifeless. Washington turned and ran back to the hall, screaming "Murder!" while trailing bloody footsteps in his wake. Frederick was quick to respond: Thinking that his brother was being attacked, he bounded down the stairs before entering the room and performing a cursory examination of the body for himself. He then rejoined his brother, and the pair hurtled down the stairs heading to the busy streets outside—both brothers later recalled noticing that the front door of the house had been left partially open.

Together they created a great ruckus in the street, screaming "Help! Police! Murder!" Although it was only a little after 6:00 a.m., the Nathans lived at the corner of Fifth Avenue and Twenty-third Street, in one of the most affluent and busiest neighborhoods in New York City. Among the passersby alerted to their screams was Officer John Magnum, assigned to patrol the neighborhood. Magnum was quickly persuaded to return with the Nathan brothers to their house to see the body. Upon closer examination, they discovered their father's body was still warm, prompting Washington to run back downstairs to the street, this time yelling for a doctor. Directly across the street from the Nathans' mansion stood the luxurious Fifth Avenue Hotel, an elite social, cultural, and political hub at the time, and its resident doctor was summoned. Sadly, the doctor confirmed what had been become increasingly evident to those on the scene: Benjamin Nathan was dead, presumably the victim of foul play.

## An Unlikely Victim

Benjamin Nathan was a capitalist and stockbroker who, by his mid-forties, had amassed enough wealth to semiretire—the stock exchange was always there for him to dabble with—and spend his later years focusing on other priorities, like health and family. At the time of his murder, he was fifty-seven and, having recovered from a lingering illness a few years earlier, was reportedly in the prime of his life; he was described as being a large, robust, attractive man. It was said that he was upright in business, steadfast in friendships, and kind in his ways—almost without an enemy in the world. While he was known particularly for contributing to Jewish charities, his goodwill extended to all mankind, with one close friend remarking, "It would be impossible to estimate the extent of the circle on which his sad death falls as an absolute calamity."

BENJAMIN NATHAN.

THE *JOURNAL AND TRIBUNE*

Nathan came from money, with his family's roots dating back to America's colonial times, and was esteemed in society circles for his generosity, notably helping to establish Mount Sinai Hospital and gifting an estimated $500,000 to the hospital and other charities throughout his lifetime; he was serving as president of the board of directors of the hospital at the time of his death. The New York Stock Exchange, which Nathan had been a member of for more than thirty years, issued resolutions expressing sympathy for the family and closed its doors on the morning of August 1 so that members could attend Benjamin's funeral. The NYSE's flags were set at half-mast to honor his passing.

## A Shocking Scene

The Nathan brothers' cries of alarm had attracted a multitude of interested parties to their house, including friends, relatives, and complete strangers who just happened to be in the vicinity. Within a few hours, the crime scene had been secured by the police, with Superintendent John Jourdan himself arriving on the site before 9:00 a.m.

As found at the scene, the body of Benjamin Nathan was lying on its back, slightly inclined to the left. His head was straight, while his right leg extended out across the doorway and his left was drawn up, jammed against the door. His hands were extended outward, with the right one laying a little higher up than the left; both hands were partially open, not tightly clenched. He was wearing only a nightshirt, smeared with blood from head to foot.

It appeared that his skull had been crushed by a blunt instrument; his face and eyes had been bruised, and there were two large wounds on his head. Both of his hands also had bruises, and some of his fingers were broken. Blood and bits of brain had soaked into the carpet and splattered across the wall dividing the two rooms, indicating his death had come after a violent struggle.

In Nathan's bedroom, a gray coat, a pair of trousers, and a white shirt were draped over a chair near the window opposite the bed; the clothes had a few spots of blood on them. The bed had a somewhat impromptu feel to it; four mattresses were hastily piled one on top of the other, as Nathan's return from his country estate had intruded upon work being done on his quarters. On the bed was a wooden drawer that had been removed from a safe in the office. The drawer contained only a few French and American coins and a handful of documents. On a table by the bed were his eyeglasses, which he reportedly struggled to see without.

Past the body, into the office, the shutter on the desk had been left open, with a few papers left scattered on the desk's surface. The chair was upturned and had marks on it, suggesting it had played a part in the struggle; the bottom of the chair was streaked with blood and contained matted hair.

The safe in the office was found open, its drawer discarded on the bed in the other room. Nathan's sons later testified that their father rarely kept much in the way of valuables or cash there; these he left in his offices downtown. He usually kept only a few bonds in his home safe—some of these were found thrown about on the bed—and other paperwork, perhaps a little petty cash to pay the servants' salaries. Washington found the key, which his father usually kept on his person, still in the safe's lock.

Missing from the body, it was later learned, were a set of three 1¾ carat stud diamonds embedded in Nathan's shirt and his large Jurgensen's gold hunting-case watch, with an accompanying stem winder to which was attached a heavy gold link chain with two seals, one of which was a monogram comprising the letters B.N.

Perhaps the most significant piece of evidence had been discovered by Washington Nathan as he returned to the street for the second time to call out for medical assistance. On his way back down the stairs, he noticed an iron rod approximately two feet long and an inch and a half thick lying on the marble floor near the front door. The rod's ends were flattened and turned down at right angles. Washington was sure he had never seen it before. He pointed the suspicious item out to Officer Magnum, who was accompanying him. Magnum quickly took possession of the rod, which was later identified as an "iron dog"—a tool used by carpenters employed at sea to caulk and clamp ship planks with oakum, a binding consisting of hemp rope and tar. The dog had blood and hair smeared along its curve.

## FINAL DAYS AND HOURS

Benjamin Nathan had been spending the better part of the summer vacationing with his family at their country estate in New Jersey. He returned to his Fifth Avenue home on July 28 intending to honor the anniversary of his mother's death the following morning by attending services with his sons at their synagogue. That afternoon he attended to some business downtown, with Washington assisting him with a stock purchase. Later that evening he joined his two sons for a visit at the home of Rabbi Julius Lyons, who was also his brother-in-law. Washington was the first to leave the Lyons residence, around 7:30 p.m. Frederick said goodnight to his aunt and uncle and departed a short time after, while Benjamin stayed until a little after 9:00 p.m.

It was around midnight when Frederick returned home. As was his custom, he stopped at his father's room on the second floor to check on him. His father was still awake and offered him a glass of ice water from a pitcher he had on his bedside table; he also asked if Washington was home yet. Frederick declined the water and said he didn't think Washington had returned because the key wasn't left in the front door—the Nathans had developed a system by which the second-to-last person to come home in the evening would take the key to the front door from a nearby drawer and insert it into the lock, leaving it for the last person home to lock up before he went to bed. Benjamin and Frederick bid each other goodnight, and Frederick retired to his bedroom on the third floor.

It wasn't too much later that Washington returned from his night out, finding the key left by his brother and securing the house. He also went to check on his father but found the door closed and the light off, so continued on to his bedroom, also on the third floor.

Seemingly, the night passed undisturbed, as neither Frederick nor Washington—nor Mrs. Ann Kelly and her son, William, who lived and worked in the house as domestic servants and were the only other inhabitants of the Nathan home on the night of Thursday, July 28—heard anything that disturbed them during the night. However unlikely, they all must have slept through what the crime scene indicated was a brutal struggle that ended with Benjamin Nathan's demise.

## Botched Burglary

All of the early evidence pointed toward Benjamin Nathan's murder resulting from a burglary attempt that had ended in disaster. Based on the testimony of his sons, Nathan was in his bed at midnight and presumably asleep by 12:15 a.m. When discovered, the body had already begun to grow cold, and its spilled blood had had time to coagulate, putting the time of death between 12:30 and 3:30 a.m. The detectives conceived of a scenario where a burglar, or burglars, had broken in to ransack the place, waking Nathan in the process. As indicated by the splattering of blood on the wall, carpet, and pile of clothes, it seemed that a fatal struggle had ensued, likely involving the iron dog that was discarded by the front door, almost as an afterthought, as the killer fled.

The detectives and press debated whether the perpetrators were "professional burglars" or more of the "loafer" variety, taking advantage of an opportunity that had arisen. Superintendent Jourdan believed it was the work of a lone professional, citing the lack of a firearm, which a burglar would not carry, leaving only the dog as an improvised murder weapon. However, the fact that a violent altercation had occurred and the discovery of the iron dog—useless as a burglar's tool to pry open windows, doors, or safes—argued for the culprit being an amateur; an experienced burglar would always seek to flee whenever possible, which he would have had ample opportunity to do in this instance. Regardless of whether the killer was a seasoned professional who had strategically planned the operation, perhaps botched only by Nathan's unexpected return from New Jersey, or an opportunistic miscreant who got in over his head, an obvious question remained: How did they gain access to the house?

The Nathans' four-story high-stoop brownstone mansion, situated across the street from the Fifth Avenue Hotel, was enormous. The kitchen and laundry

FIFTH AVE. HOTEL. 5TH AVE. COR. 23RD ST.

WIKIMEDIA

rooms were located in the English basement, while the first floor had spacious halls, butler pantries, a parlor, and a dining room. The layout of the second floor, where Benjamin Nathan's body was found, was described by the press as "peculiar": The stairway opened up to a long, sweeping hall that ran more than half the floor lengthwise. Leading off from this room was the office, or library, which Nathan's legs were extending out of when the body was found, while the rest of his body was prone in the large reception room that was serving as his bedroom. The middle of the floor consisted of numerous closets, bathrooms, toilet rooms, and dressing rooms, while Mrs. Kelly's bedroom and adjoining quarters, paralleling those of the Nathans' in the front of the house, took up the rear of the floor. Frederick and Washington had bedrooms on the third floor, while William Kelly had a room on the fourth.

There were two main entryways into the house: the primary, front door and a back door leading into the basement. On the night in question, both brothers were sure that they had secured the front door, specifically recalling their family custom of locking the door in stages determined by the order in which they returned home. The basement, housing the kitchen and laundry rooms, was

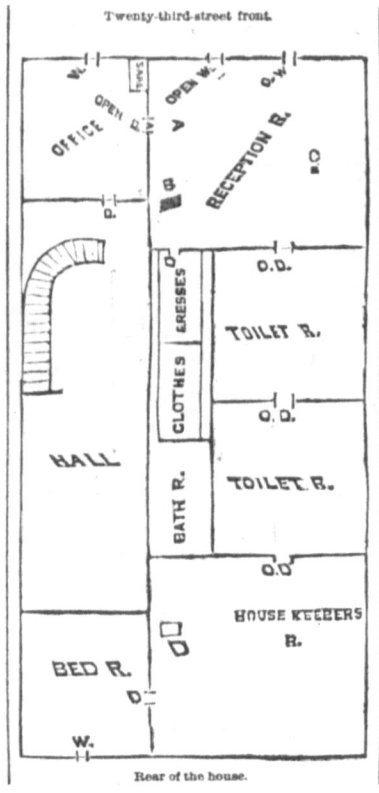

Second floor
NEW YORK TIMES

largely the purview of the domestic servants, and the back door had lately been secured by Mrs. Kelly and her son. They were sure that the back door had been secured that evening, and Mrs. Kelly later testified at the inquest that soon after the body was discovered, she went down to the basement and found the door still closed and locked. Additionally, one of the detectives who had arrived on the scene early said there were no signs of forced entry on any of the windows or doors of the home.

Although only the Nathans and the Kellys had slept in the house that night, a complicating variable was that in recent days access to the house had been practically unfettered as a parade of carpenters, plumbers, masons, and general laborers had been in and out trying to finish the upgrades and repairs while the Nathans were away; in the day before the murder alone, two carpenters, a mason, and a laborer had been working on the house. When the men were questioned, the general consensus emerged that they usually entered the premises via the basement in the back, admitted by Mrs. Kelly or her son, although occasionally they had gone in the front door. Despite the security system in place, the men reported that at times the door had been left open, such as when William Kelly was sweeping the sidewalk.

One carpenter recalled coming to work a little late one morning, and after Mrs. Kelly let him in, he inquired if his fellow worker had shown up yet. She said no, and he went off to work, waiting for his comrade to arrive. After some time had passed, he returned to their common work hall, where he was told his friend had left for work hours ago. He returned to the Nathans' and found his friend on a different floor in a far corner, where he had been working since arriving early that morning—his presence had been completely unknown to the carpenter or anyone else in the huge mansion.

The unique architecture of the Nathans' luxurious home, one of the most elegant and spacious private residences in the city, also helped solve another mystery lingering around the murder. Detectives were initially baffled as to how the other four inhabitants sleeping in the house that night were not disturbed by what presumably had been a violent struggle, based on the splattered blood and upturned furniture found at the scene of the crime. However, upon testing the scenario by re-creating the sound of Benjamin Nathan's hypothetical fight to his death, police discovered that it was impossible to hear any sound at all from the other bedrooms in the house.

## Witnesses Emerge

Police tracked down two witnesses who had passed by the house in the early hours of the morning, both with promising nuggets of information. Patrick Devoy, a waiter at Ford & Kessinger's on Fifth Avenue, was returning home from a late shift and remembered passing by the Nathans' at around 12:30 a.m. when he saw a closed carriage parked a few houses down. Devoy saw a man lying in the coach and asked him to move along but received no reply. After he arrived home, his wife informed him that the carriage had been there since 10:30 p.m., as the evening storm raged. Devoy had trouble getting to sleep; finally, around 1:30 a.m. he saw a man abruptly mount the box and drive off rapidly in the direction of Broadway.

Devoy's story seemed credible, and investigators focused on tracking down the mysterious inhabitants of the late-night carriage, calling upon private livery stables in search of the suspicious coach. However, the lead lost its energy when it was revealed that the building the mysterious carriage was parked outside of was a "house of ill repute" and that the presence of carriages at odd hours there was not uncommon—Devoy and his wife were only housesitting and didn't know the neighborhood all that well.

More impactful was the testimony of John Nies, a newsboy who had been delivering papers in the vicinity of the Nathans' around 5:00 a.m. Nies remembered coming up to the Nathans' front stoop that morning intending to stop there and fold his papers—the steps leading to the front door of the Nathans' were sheltered by a portico, which had a projecting roof that served as a shield when it rained, as it had that morning. However, upon approaching the front steps, he noticed the front door was ajar, and so he quickly moved on to find another dry spot for his work, not wanting to be chastised by an early-rising maid or butler for trespassing.

Nies's testimony established that the killers had likely departed by the front door sometime before 5:00 a.m., and Officer Magnum believed he had checked the Nathans' front door and found it secure at 1:00 a.m. The detectives were closing in on the time of death, but this did little to facilitate the solving of the crime. Believing in the burglar theory, Superintendent Jourdan and his team focused their efforts on three priorities: determining where the iron dog had come from, finding the watch and diamonds taken from Nathan's shirt, and figuring out how the killer had entered and exited the house.

Police provided descriptions of the missing diamonds and watch to all jewelers, secondhand shops, and pawnbrokers, who were told to be on the lookout. And yet their efforts proved futile. With the question of how the killer could have possibly gained access to the house still lingering, some newspapers began proposing alternatives to the burglar theory, explanations that also answered the question of how the killer had gotten inside: They were already there.

## Someone in the House

Most of the Nathan family was still in their country home in New Jersey when the murder occurred and largely managed to avoid the spotlight of press coverage; Frederick, and Washington especially, were not so lucky. Washington quickly became a leading suspect of the tabloids. After all, it was only his word that he had arrived home sometime after midnight, when everyone else, including his father, was in bed asleep. Washington was also the one who discovered the body in the morning as he went downstairs for a glass of ice water—it would have been child's play to stage a robbery out of the scene by simply rifling through the contents of the safe. And when he was seen by Officer Magnum and the other witnesses who rushed to respond to the Nathan brothers' cries in the street, his nightshirt was soaked with his father's blood. Furthermore, the only blood found outside of the immediate area of the crime scene was that of Washington's bloody footprints, trailing away from the body out into the stairway.

At the time of the murder, Washington Nathan was twenty-one years old, the sixth child in a family of eight. Washington was living at home, as were most of his siblings. He was employed as a Wall Street broker at Wright & Nathan, the firm he had started with money provided by his father. Although the business was not terribly successful, he testified that he was earning enough to pay his bills.

Washington was the only person of note to appear on the first day of a hurriedly put together coroner's inquest and was reportedly still in an agitated state when questioned, just two days after finding his father's body. The press reported that the inquest itself was "irregularly conducted," with witness testimony at times being incorrectly transcribed or not recorded by the coroner at all. Faced with such criticism and with the first day yielding little useful information, investigators halted the proceedings to allow themselves a chance to review the facts and chase down leads. When the inquest resumed a week later, Washington returned to the stand, calmer now, not hurried and anxious as he had been the first day, despite increasingly probing questions from the coroner that delved into matters beyond the strict events of the murder to include sensitive areas of Washington's private life.

Testimony from Frederick and Washington revealed that their father had been very generous to all of his adult children. Although they weren't given an allowance, their father never refused them money when asked, perhaps only gently chiding them about being more responsible or inquiring into their affairs. Washington had most recently received $5,000 from his father for his nascent broker business the previous year and had already repaid $1,000. It was revealed that on occasions, such as when he was lending out money, Benjamin would lightly criticize Washington for some of his lifestyle choices, such as staying out too late at night or not being more prudent with his money, but those who testified emphasized there was never any lasting ill will from these conversations. Family and friends confirmed that Washington and his father were on good terms.

From questioning about his activities on the night before the murder, it was revealed that Washington had been quite busy. After leaving his father and brother at his uncle's, he strolled around the neighborhood a bit before meeting up with a friend named Mr. Gand, who accompanied him to the St. James Hotel for a glass of sherry. There he met up with a Mr. Arnold, two ladies, and another gentleman, all of whom then went on to dine at DelMonico's before returning later to the St. James. A stroll down Fifth Avenue followed, during which Washington ran into an associate named Mr. Wolf. It was now nearly 11:00 p.m., and he took a cab to a friend's house on Fourteenth Street, where he stayed for an hour or so until he went home.

Washington's otherwise detailed account of what he did after leaving his uncle's was notable for initially omitting the identity of the friend whose home he had visited just before the end of his evening. This was rectified when Clara Dale was called to the stand to confirm Washington's story, which she did under brief and concise questioning on August 11. Although it was not revealed, or even alluded to, during the inquest, it was later learned that Washington had paid for the pleasure of Miss Dale's company, helping to absolve him of his father's murder but also casting a long shadow over his reputation at a time when violating social norms and mores often resulted in severe and lasting consequences.

Simply by virtue of arriving home earlier in the evening and being second downstairs the fateful morning, Frederick was spared much of the accusatory innuendo from the press that his brother faced; he also suffered less probing into his personal life at the inquest. Not as fortunate in this regard was the other male sleeping in the house that night, William Kelly, the housekeeper's son. Ann Kelly was sixty years old and unlikely to be able to physically overcome Benjamin Nathan even if she did have a motive, which she did not. However, investigators seemed more interested in her son, who was described in early reports as "a very simple fellow."

William Kelly was twenty-four years old and a veteran of the Union Army, having served during the Civil War. After the war ended, he held numerous jobs in a variety of professions, working in a hat factory for about a year, assisting a plumber with gas fittings, working for a silversmith, and toiling in a boiler shop for another year. Kelly never learned a trade or successfully rose above a supporting role in any of his jobs; for one reason or another, nothing worked out long term. Thus, he had ended up living at the Nathans' along with his mother. He received $8 a month for his army pension but had no regular wage. He earned money doing chores and running errands—sweeping the sidewalk, delivering documents, for example—for members of the household.

Although there was no direct evidence pointing toward him, and he lacked any obvious motive for the murder, Kelly did have the means, his bedroom being only two floors above Benjamin's. Kelly took the stand on August 11 and was questioned aggressively by the coroner and jury. Previously Washington had testified that when he first woke, he heard footsteps from the floor above; Kelly explained that he had been up already, as his usual habit was to rise early and collect the shoes from the hallways for cleaning. The rest of the questioning was lengthy but generally proved ineffective, as Kelly's accounting of his activities from the day before, up through the morning when the body was found, was routine and verified by others.

The largest stone upturned at the inquest had to do with Kelly's time in the army, which he was clearly uncomfortable talking about. For reasons not publicly disclosed, he had gone to Lawrence, Massachusetts, when he enlisted, and had done so under an alias, James Watson. It was further disclosed that George Deagan and Patrick Calahan, the gentlemen who recruited Kelly into signing up, were suspected of operating a "bounty jumping" racket, in which men would enlist and collect the enrollment bonus only to quickly desert, often going on to pull the same con in a different location. Kelly was able to provide documentation showing he had served to the end of the war and was honorably discharged.

As the inquest ended, Washington Nathan and William Kelly were seemingly absolved of Benjamin Nathan's murder, although both emerged bruised and battered in society's court of public opinion. On September 14, the final coroner's report stated, "Mr. Benjamin Nathan came to his death from wounds inflicted upon his head by an instrument known as a 'dog,' in the hands of a person or persons to this jury unknown." Over the years, random rumors and confessions from prisoners in jail would point to a new suspect being the culprit, but all lacked any real evidence and came to nothing in the end.

## Tragic Legacy

In all likelihood, the murder was committed by a burglar unexpectedly caught in the act by the recently returned owner of the house. The work being done on the house provided ample opportunity for any of the workers, their associates, or even random opportunistic persons who, upon observing the state of the house, would be able to gain access and hide away in one of the many rooms of its cavernous four floors and basement. One of the detectives stated at the inquest, "There are plenty of places for a man to conceal himself in the house; there are closets and wardrobes and such like I never saw more in a house." Sometime after midnight, when everything had settled, the killer probably took their chance, only to be confronted by Benjamin, whose efforts to defend his home had fatal consequences.

Beyond the tragedy that was the murder of Benjamin Nathan, whose killer was never found, the crime haunted the Nathan family, and Washington Nathan in particular, for years to come. Washington was never able to escape the cloud cast upon him at the inquest and in the press. His habits of alcohol abuse and womanizing continued in the ensuing years, culminating in him being shot behind the ear by a scorned lover who accused him of owing her money; a bit of the bullet remained lodged in his neck for the rest of his life because the attending doctor thought it could do no harm. He spent his final days overseas, living in a suburb of London, having burned through much of his inheritance, reportedly largely friendless. He died at the age of forty-three, with his final thoughts and words still occupied by his father's murder, declaring his innocence one last time.

The Nathan family descendants of today look back at the unsolved murder of Benjamin Nathan as a turning point, when their family fell from prominence and never fully recovered. To this day, Washington Nathan is remembered as the black sheep of the family.

## 2

# The New York Ripper

### *New York City*

It's early on the morning of Friday, November 9, 1888, and Mary Jane Kelly is sloshed. Again. Tall and stout, with blonde hair and blue eyes, Kelly has fallen on hard times since leaving Ireland for London four years earlier. True, she's peddling her wares at an East End brothel, but somehow she's always strapped for cash. Her rent is six weeks overdue. Tonight she hits up buddy George Hutchinson for a sixpence, but George is unemployed and broke. A dapper thirtysomething bloke with a dark mustache approaches. They exchange pleasantries. Kelly mentions that she's lost her handkerchief; he presents her with one of his own, bright red.

"All right, my dear, come along," Kelly says. "You will be comfortable."

They amble on over to 13 Miller's Court. The man tugs his hat down over his eyes as they pass Hutchinson.

Mary Kelly is never seen alive again.

Later that morning, her body is discovered lying nude on her bed, horribly mutilated. Her abdomen and thighs are severed, the abdominal cavity emptied of viscera. Her breasts have been hacked off beyond recognition. Her uterus, kidneys, and one breast all lie under her head, the other breast by her right foot. Her liver sits between her feet, her intestines by the right side of her body, and her spleen by the left.

This is the work of Jack the Ripper, who terrorized London's Whitechapel district from late August to November 1888. Kelly was his fifth and final canonical victim (though some reports attribute six additional murders to him). The Ripper's identity was never definitively uncovered.

There is no conclusive evidence that Jack the Ripper ever extended his killing spree to New York, but some Ripperologists theorize that he did. The murder they point to happened three years after Mary Kelly's gruesome death, in Manhattan's scabrous Sixth Ward, home to the notorious Five Points. The victim, Carrie Brown, was a sixty-something dipsomaniac brothel worker known as Old Shakespeare because she could recite entire passages of the Bard's work by heart, and while a man was convicted of the crime, he was eventually pardoned by the governor of New York, and not a soul on earth seems to think he was truly guilty.

## Murder at the East River Hotel

Sometime between 10:30 and 11:00 p.m. on the rainy night of Thursday, April 23, 1891, the old woman checks into the squalid East River Hotel on Manhattan's waterfront accompanied by a fair-skinned man with light-colored hair and a mustache, about thirty years old; five feet, eight inches tall; and slim, with a long, sharp nose. He's wearing a dark-brown cutaway coat, black trousers, and an old black derby hat with a dented crown. The man signs the register "C. Knick" and tells Mary Miniter, the assistant housekeeper, that the old woman is his wife.

"Aw!" Brown says, "can't I have some beer?"

The man nods, handing a dime to Miniter.

"Beer or mixed ale?" Miniter asks.

"Mixed ale," answers the old woman.

Miniter fetches a pail of mixed ale from the bar and hands it to the woman.

Brown and the man ascend the narrow, uneven stairs to Room 31, a corner room.

At about nine o'clock the following morning, Miniter sends an employee upstairs to "clear the floors." Arriving at Room 31, he knocks. Nobody answers. He struggles with the door, managing to open it slightly. Inside he sees the woman's twisted, lifeless body lying on the bed, naked from the armpits down.

It is 175 years and one day since the death of William Shakespeare.

Authorities, summoned to the scene, determine that the woman had been strangled, stabbed, and disemboweled. The murderer had left his mark with two carved crosses: one on the woman's back left hip in jagged lines more than a foot long and the other on the wall. A white cotton shirt is wrapped so tightly around her head that the coroner has to cut it off. Parts of her intestines are missing, and the left ovary is completely severed. Blood is everywhere, on the sheets, quilts, bedstead, and floor and smeared in finger marks on the limbs. The knife used to commit the murder is thrust beneath the woman's right thigh, the bloody handle projecting.

C. Knick, on the other hand, is nowhere to be found, having slipped undetected into the streets of Manhattan overnight.

## Arrest and Trial
The old woman's real identity is believed to have been Ellen Caroline Montgomery, a native Liverpudlian once married to Salem, Massachusetts, sea captain James Brown, who had either died or deserted her over her obsessive boozing. She'd turned to prostitution and been arrested twenty-eight times for drunkenness.

Brown's death merited a brief mention in Herbert Asbury's 1927 book, *The Gangs of New York: An Informal History of the Underworld*, which labels her an "old hag" who claimed to hail from aristocracy in England, where she had once been a celebrated actress.

Brown's grisly murder and the fact that she was a lady of the night led to speculation that Jack the Ripper had fled England for New York, rumors New York authorities hardly discouraged. Before Brown's murder, New York City

Carrie Brown
PHOTO COURTESY OF NEW ENGLAND HISTORY SOCIETY

Police inspector Thomas Byrnes had taunted his London counterparts over their failure to apprehend the Ripper, boasting that anyone who went about committing the kinds of crimes the Ripper did in New York would have been locked up within thirty-six hours. Perhaps the Ripper had taken Byrnes up on his dare? Asked if he believed Jack the Ripper had killed Old Shakespeare, the coroner responded, "I believe this case is the same as those of London. . . . I do not see any reason to suppose that the crime may not have been committed by the fiend of London." To this day, some Ripperologists cite the Brown murder as the work of Polish barber-surgeon Severin Klosowski, a Ripper suspect who also went by George Chapman. Klosowski had moved to Jersey City, New Jersey, in 1891, though possibly not until after Brown was murdered. Another possibility, suggested by writer James Tully, is that Brown's killer was James Kelly, another Ripper suspect, who may have traveled to New York after the Ripper murders in London stopped. Neither of these suggestions is considered likely.

The press jumped all over Brown's murder, pressuring Byrnes to crack the case. Within twenty-four hours, police had two suspects locked up and more on deck, though they never were able to track down their prime target, the mysterious C. Knick. The first arrest of significance was of a penniless French Algerian vagrant named Ameer Ben Ali (aka George Frank or Frenchy), a tall, dark-complexioned man with a long, slim nose, a black mustache, black hair, and a notorious reputation who, unfortunately for him, had also spent the night of April 23 at the East River Hotel, in Room 33, across the hall from Brown.

By April 30, police had conveniently changed their story and insisted that Ben Ali was the man they'd wanted all along. Their scenario was that Ali had entered Brown's room sometime after C. Knick left, then murdered and robbed Brown before returning to his own room. Charged with first-degree murder, Ben Ali, who spoke little English, was put on trial in July 1901 and didn't make the greatest of impressions. As Ripperologist Richard Jones recounted in 2019, "When the prisoner shuffled into court, he looked more like a wild animal than like a man. His black hair and beard were matted. His tiny black eyes had a wolfish glare. He was almost six feet in height, but his powerful shoulders were bent and his long, lean legs crooked at the knee. His arms were abnormally long. With their gnarled and lengthy hands, whose knotty fingers ended in claw-like nails, they suggested the arms of a gorilla. A dozen of the physical abnormalities enumerated by criminologists as stigmata of degeneracy were apparent in 'Frenchy.'"

According to Jones: "Never was there a more dramatic moment in the old General Session Court-House than when 'Frenchy' leapt from the witness chair and, raising his long hands high above his head and gazing upward, uttered cries in his wild language—cries of prayer, of protection, of frenzied appeal."

Ali's interpreter translated the outburst this way: "He calls to God and says he is innocent."

Ben Ali was convicted of second-degree murder—not first—and sentenced to life in prison. But eleven years into his sentence, he was pardoned by New York governor Benjamin Odell, who had received affidavits from, among others, reporters Jacob A. Riis and Charles Edward Russell, who had conducted their own investigations. Both pointed out that when they initially viewed the crime scene, before the coroner arrived, they hadn't seen any bloodstains in the hallway between Rooms 31 and 33, on the doors of either room, or in Ben Ali's room, contradicting police testimony. The implication was that these bloodstains, found by the police the day *after* the murder, likely had resulted from the removal of the body by the coroner. Further, police records clearly stated that there had been no blood on the doorknob or lock of Room 31 even though, according to authorities, the killer had used the key to unlock, open, and then relock the door. Police never managed to locate the key either.

It didn't help that Byrnes was forced to resign in 1895, a target of an anti-corruption crusade by Theodore Roosevelt, newly named president of the New York City Police Commission.

Following his pardon, Ben Ali was released and left for his native Algeria.

### THE "DANISH FARMHAND" THEORY

In May 1901, respectable New York City businessman George Damon and two other people swore in affidavits that a man named Frank, who had worked for Damon at his Cranford, New Jersey, home, was missing the night of the murder and came home at six the following morning in so foul a mood that his fellow farmhands avoided him like the plague. This in turn gave rise to the "Danish Farmhand" theory, as Frank was believed to be from Denmark, although possibly Sweden. Damon claimed that a week or so after Frank had bolted for places unknown, a brass key tagged "Room 31" was discovered in his bedroom along with a bloody shirt. While these affidavits played a role in Ben Ali's eventual pardon, Damon's description of Frank didn't match Mary Miniter's recollection of what C. Knick looked like, and the keys to the East River Hotel rooms were made of iron, not brass. This theory was eventually rejected by police and has since been discredited by, among others, Howard and Nina Brown, authors of *An Illustrated Encyclopedia: The 1891 Murder of Carrie Brown*.

Still, the general consensus today is that Ben Ali was innocent, the victim of a shoddy, corrupt investigation by a police force that had buckled under relentless pressure to crack the case.

Twenty-four years after Carrie Brown's death, a man claiming to be Jack the Ripper killed two young children in Lower Manhattan, triggering a wave of panic that far transcended the neighborhood.

Like his namesake, he was never caught or even identified.

## LEONORE COHN

March 19, 1915, another Friday. Around 7:00 p.m., five-year-old Leonore Cohn (sometimes spelled Leonora or Lenore), swinging a three-quart graniteware pail and singing her favorite children's song, sets out on an errand to purchase a quart of loose milk. Leonore lives with her mom, Anna, a nurse; her aunt and uncle; her cousin; and her grandparents in a walkup at 350 Third Avenue, a grimy neighborhood teeming with vagrants who pass out in the hallways of unlocked tenement buildings. Julius Pollachek, a resident of the same building, passes Leonore on the stairs on his way to a lodge meeting and can't help smiling; a precocious child, she has been nicknamed Smarty by neighbors, and the song she is singing is known to them as the "Smarty song."

Leonore's first stop is the bakery at 370 Third Avenue, where Julia Codis informs her they don't sell loose milk, so Leonore says thank you and leaves. Codis watches her walk out the door, spotting a "foreign looking" man with dark hair lingering near the exit.

*Such a little toddler to be out on an errand*, Codis thinks.

Back at her apartment, Leonore is sent out again, this time by her aunt, Molly Ecker, to a deli on East Twenty-sixth Street. Leonore enters the store still singing her song and purchases a quart of milk on credit from Mrs. Hermann Jungen, who tosses in a couple of animal crackers for free. Again she returns to her tenement building, this time with a pail full of milk. At about 7:30 p.m., Adolph Schrader and his daughter, Caroline, a playmate of Leonore's, pass her as she ascends the stairs to her flat. She smiles at them, displaying the pail of milk and a lemon-drop candy she is holding. Helen Spaengler (also spelled Spingler), whose flat is directly below the Cohns', also sees Leonore ascending the stairs toward her own door.

"Where's Bubbie?" Leonore asks, referring to Spaengler's six-year-old son. Alfred.

Leonore is about three steps from her front door. She never makes it.

At 7:45-ish, Augusta Johnson, sewing in her second-floor flat, hears a child scream. She rushes into the hallway. The stairwell is covered in shadows, and she can't make out much of anything. She stumbles, looks down at her feet. There, at the foot of the stairs, is Leonore, lying face down, her dress and coat soaked in blood. Her pail lies beside her, still filled with milk, not a drop spilt. Nearby is her handkerchief; stuck in one corner is the lemon-drop candy, still wet. In her left hand she clutches several strands of gray hair.

Anna Cohn, having rushed home from work, collapses. She'll later tell reporters, "It seems but a few days since I buried my husband, and yet it is three years. Soon after that the other baby died, and now they have taken all that I have. I don't feel so much for myself, but it is the way they did it, the way my little darling must have suffered! What agony she must have endured! How any human being, male or female, could commit such a crime I can't understand. Only an archfiend would be capable of it. I pray to God to give me the strength that I may devote my life to finding the murderer of my child or helping the police to do so."

## "A Typical Sadist Crime"

Dr. Edgar T. Ray, who performed the autopsy, determined that Leonore's abdomen had been sliced with a seven-inch-long butcher knife. A deep stab in the right side of the neck had severed the jugular vein, and there was a three-inch cut on the right side of her back. The center of the wound showed that the murderer had twisted the blade to make sure she was dead. Further, Leonore had been "criminally assaulted," a likely euphemism for sexual molestation.

Her neck was bruised on the left side, and fingernail marks were apparent on the right. Police believed the killer had waited for her in the hallway within a few steps from her apartment, seized her by the throat, strangled her to keep her quiet, then carried her down a flight of stairs, where the stabbing occurred.

"It is a typical sadist crime," the medical examiner told reporters. "It is the set of a species of lunatic well known to alienists."

"The indications are that the crime was committed by an insane man," Police Commissioner Arthur Woods added. "I will put every man I can on the case until it is solved. If necessary I shall assign every man in the detective bureau to the crime. The solution of this crime must be reached."

Soon, reports surfaced that for a month in winter, neighborhood children had been approached by a roughly dressed elderly man who offered them candy and pennies if they would accompany him. By the time police were informed, the man had vanished. The *Evening World* reported that the neighborhood was home to "all sorts of human derelicts . . . broken men . . . hobos and lazy half-criminals," adding, "All through the Ward are newly arrived Italians, Greeks and many other kinds of immigrants who float about from place to place without fixed abode or employment. . . . It is well known that among certain ignorant immigrants from the south of Europe, there is a superstitious belief that by sacrificing a little girl a man can be cured of certain complaints."

On March 22, the day of Leonore's burial, hundreds of women, many accompanied by their children, were "almost impossible to restrain" as they filed onto Third Avenue and the nearby streets, blocking traffic as they sought to console Anna Cohn, whose cries "could be heard throughout the house," according to the *Evening World*.

Police believed the killer was familiar enough with the tenement house to know what door Leonore would enter and that his appearance apparently didn't alarm her. They claimed to have two suspects in mind, both residents of the building. One, newspapers reported, was of particular interest because he was known to masquerade in women's clothing, explaining to police that he did it for fun. Police searched both 350 and 352 Third Avenue from top to bottom looking for bloodstained clothing, and while the first search turned up empty, detectives suggested to reporters that they had found exactly what they were looking for during round two. When queried about it, a high-ranking cop requesting anonymity replied, "If you should find in the tenement where this murder was committed a package of clothing containing bloodstains that could not be satisfactorily accounted for, what would be your conclusion?"

That it was time to make an arrest, reporters responded.

"We can't just do that, but such a find would suggest to us that we ought certainly to investigate the case most closely," said Woods, who overheard the conversation.

Henry Ecker, Leonore's uncle, was also convinced she knew her killer: "The man who killed her knew her. She wouldn't have let any stranger pick her up. She wouldn't have let him touch her. She'd have screamed so loud everybody in the house would have heard her.

"We'll get him yet," Ecker told the *New-York World*. "He'll give up his secret by talking. A German motto runs '*Wie gerspannen so zerommen*,' and that means 'So as the spinning, so the unraveling."

A table knife daubed in red paint was found on the roof of the tenement house the day after the suspect discovered he was being investigated. Police believed the weapon was placed there by someone hoping to divert them from the real killer, since they had searched the area multiple times. The knife was found by Richard Ecker, the girl's cousin.

Police apprehended suspects left and right, but none could be tied to Leonore's murder. At a police conference on March 23, Deputy Commissioner Frank Lord said, "When I hit, I want to do it with such force that it will be felt. I will be greatly disappointed if something good does not happen tomorrow."

But nothing did happen. And then, on March 24, six-year-old Julia Hawkins of Brooklyn was rescued by her ten-year-old brother, Henry, from a man attacking her in the cellar of their home. Doctors said Julia would be "ill for a long time," and her mother announced she would organize the women of her church to search for the man and protect children in the neighborhood.

On March 27, a letter appeared in the *New York Times* from a woman who signed her name "An East Side Mother":

> Within five short blocks of the scene of Lenore's murder, surrounded by hundreds of unknown people, I watch and pray for the safety of every child in the streets, knowing that the degenerate is still at large. Today, my little girl was late for lunch. I rushed down the stairs, into the street, around the corner, and I saw her coming—happy, entirely unmindful of the fear in her mother's heart. Through my tears of thankfulness I saw other women, all asking the same questions at once: "Why were you late?" "What kept you?" as they seized the little hands and hurried their children along. All over our neighborhood any one can see the terror that will flare out at the least little thing. Can any man tell us why this should be.

## LETTERS FROM "JACK THE RIPPER"

Soon after Leonore's murder, Anna Cohn began receiving letters from an individual claiming to be the killer. The first of these letters arrived on March 29, signed "Jack the Ripper":

> MRS. COHN:
>
> Dear Madam: Your family had better call off the police and detectives. They are a lot of rag-pickers. They could not clear up this case or any other in a hundred years. They are going about this job in their usual thick-headed way, accusing an innocent man wrongfully.
>
> I did the job. If you persist in your present methods and conduct I will kill a couple more of your family.

On the other side of the sheet, the writer scrawled that the Ecker family had "guilty knowledge about the murder." At the bottom of the page were these words:

"This is my signature,
H. B. Richmond,
Brooklyn, N.Y."

On the opposite side of the sheet was what the *Evening World* described as a "vile drawing," along with the words "This is my business."

Within days, Anna Cohn received two more letters. One stated that the writer knew of the murder, had been implicated in it, and was willing to share valuable information for $100, to be left at a Harlem saloon. He threatened to murder again if the money was not delivered. On the reverse side were a skull and crossbones, a black hand, and a dagger. The second letter, again signed "H. B. Richmond, Jack the Ripper," and written on the stationery of the New York Republican Club, read:

> Dear Madam: This is the second letter I am writing you. I know that you have received the first one. You had better call off these ragpicker detectives, for they are accusing innocent people. I am going to commit the worst murder in New York and see if they can get me. I am always in the neighborhood and see their moves and hear the news.

On April 29, police arrested twentysomething Edward Richman and charged him with sending the letters to Anna Cohn. But he, too, was cleared of any involvement in Leonore's murder. And two days after his arrest, Anna Cohn received another letter:

> Dear Mrs. Cohn: Just a line to let you know that the person that is accused of writing letters to you is innocent. I am the fellow that wrote you the letters, and as I said before a man that keeps his ears open and mouth shut will always get along and never get caught. Some day thats if I get the chair I may confess. But as long as I am out they can never get me. Kindly give the enclosed letter to the police and tell them I wrote it.
>
> —H.B RICHMOND, Jack-the-ripper

Inside was a second envelope, labeled "Give this to the police." Inside that envelope was another letter:

Why don't you drop this case? You know that man can't get me in 100 years from now so its no youse in sirchen for me. I am a wise guy you know but wise guys never get caught. You may think that I am a fool to write you But I am writing just to show that I aint afraid. Mr. Richmond [sic] is innocent of the letter which you accuse him of writing to Mrs. Cohn. I am the one that wrote all of them. As I told you in one of my letters that is going to be the biggest murders to be committed in N.Y. that was ever known. Now do you see I am true.

—H.B RICHMOND, JACK-THE-RIPPER

Police suspected Richman had written these latest letters to divert suspicion from himself for the earlier missives, but the fingerprints were blurred, and police never uncovered any evidence linking him to the latest threats.

And then, on May 3, the New York Ripper struck again.

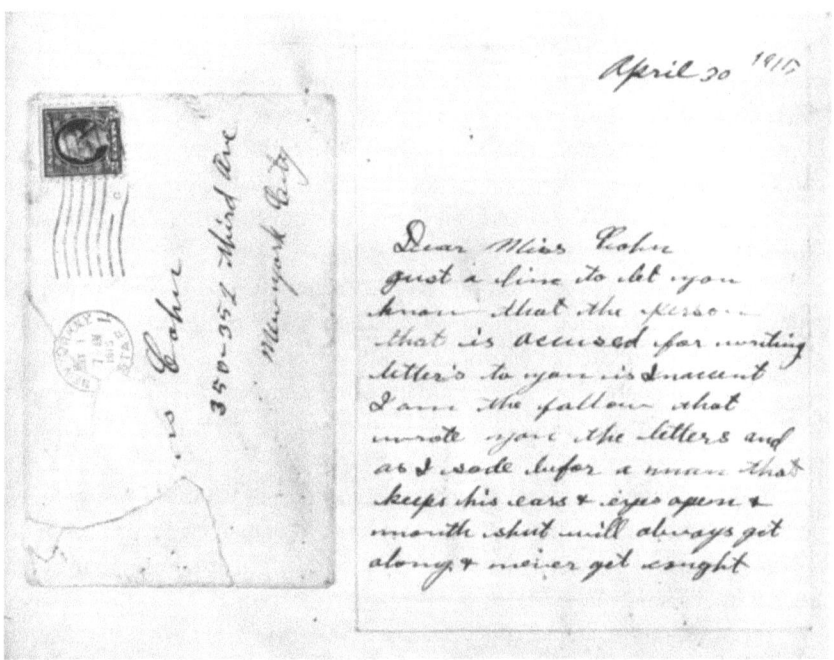

Anna Cohn letter
PHOTO COURTESY OF THE *EVENING WORLD*

## CHARLES MURRAY

Four-year-old Charles Murray and his five-year-old buddy, Frank Damico, are enjoying a game of hide-and-seek in the backyard of their tenement building at 270 First Avenue on Monday, May 3. His eight-year-old sister, Mamie, buys him an ice cream cone, then heads upstairs to their flat. Just before 7:30 p.m., Frank's parents call him in.

Minutes later, twelve-year-old Bernard Gaffney's mother, Mary, sends him to the backyard to dump the trash. On his way, he spots Charles under the stairway between the first and second floor, motionless, and lets out a scream. He runs back inside to tell his mom, who accompanies him to the hallway.

"It looks like someone's under there," Bernard says. "I know him by his white stockings. He must be asleep. He doesn't move."

"No, he isn't asleep," his mother replies. "Run. Tell his father something has happened."

What's happened is this: Charles Murray's abdomen ripped open with two long knife slashes, crisscrossed over the stomach. His liver is missing.

Nicholas Murray, a plate printer, and his wife dash down the stairs. A crowd has gathered. How could this have happened? Nobody had heard a single suspicious sound, even though the murder was committed during the dinner hour, when most of the families were home. Adolph Lesser had been sitting out in front of his hardware store with members of his family, with the door into the hallway where the murder took place wide open. Cigar store owner Samuel Schwarz and his wife, Celia, had been positioned on the other side of the wall separating their apartment from the hallway,

Based on the time and location of the crime, the age of the victims, the type of weapon used, and the nature of the wounds, authorities are adamant that Leonore Cohn and Charles Murray were killed by the same man.

"This is undoubtedly the work of the same murderer who killed Leonore Cohn," Lieutenant Patrick Gildea says. "The crime has the same distinguishing features."

Inspector Joseph Faurot concurs: "The murderer of Charles Murray is evidently the same person who killed Leonore Cohn. The man evidently lives in the neighborhood and is an arch-fiend. I would give my right arm to get him, but he has left us absolutely no clue."

The most promising of the "no clues" was that Charles's sister Mamie claimed to have seen a "foreign man" fleeing the hallway after Charles's body was found.

PHOTO COURTESY OF THE *EVENING WORLD*

She described him as dark with a dark mustache, comparing him to a detective standing nearby: about thirty-five years old, six feet tall, wearing a black hat and black clothes. Several suspects were brought in for identification, and despite the hue and cry over the killing, in each case Mamie—to her unending credit—insisted she couldn't be certain if police had apprehended the right man. Before long, authorities came to suspect she had fabricated her story.

In the wake of the two murders and seemingly endless reports of children being attacked on the streets by vagrants, mass hysteria gripped the neighborhood. Then, more bad news: Just minutes before Charles Murray's death, a man had tried to drag six-year-old Louise Neidig into a hallway as she was playing in front of a bakery shop on First Avenue, about five blocks from the Murray house. Had it not been for her screams, which frightened him away, she—and not Charles—might have been his next victim.

"A man came up to me and took me by the arm," Louise said. "He was a little man, and he had a diamond pin. He said, 'Where do you live, little girl?' I did not speak to him. Then he knocked me in the doorway and I screamed and he ran away."

On May 6, thousands gathered near the Murray home as the funeral for Charles was about to start. Twenty policemen stood by to maintain order. More than half the crowd was under ten years of age. Edward Carlson, a twenty-two-year-old unemployed valet, drew attention when he stared at Charles's face as he lay in the coffin. As the cortege lined up to head for the cemetery, Carlson approached the hearse several times, then backed into the crowd and walked around the block, always returning to the spot where the cortege was forming. Alarmed by his "most peculiar" behavior, as the *Evening World* phrased it, two cops tailed him back to his rooming house on East Fifty-third Street; when they interviewed him, he jack-rabbited over the balustrade into the hall below, lacerating his head and face. Still, police concluded he had nothing to do with the Murray or Cohn murder. Mrs. Murray and her sister Kitty Sumpter spotted another man acting strangely during the funeral, whom they believed fit Mamie's description of the man she saw fleeing the building in the wake of her brother's murder.

"This afternoon a strange man, an Italian, came into the parlor," Mrs. Murray said. "He did not look at my boy. He stared about the room. His actions were so suspicious, and I was so wrought up that I told him if I thought he was the murderer of my boy he would never leave the room alive. He leered at me and left, followed by my two sisters.

"At First Avenue, near Tenth Street, Kitty demanded that a patrolman, whose number is 1236 and who is an Italian, arrest the man, but he refused, saying he knew the man as an honest fruit peddler. Kitty came back to the house, and distracted at the thought of a possible clue being left [un]investigated, I rushed down the avenue . . . I met the same officer. He still refused to do anything for us. We searched until we found the man, and then the officer agreed to take him before little Mamie. Mamie could not identify him except to say that he looked like the man, and after the detectives questioned him and took his name he went away."

Departure for the cemetery was delayed more than an hour until Mrs. Murray, crying hysterically, could control herself sufficiently to let the casket be closed. Four of his friends acted as pallbearers, led by Bernard Gaffney, who had discovered the body.

## Panic in the Streets

Faurot was taking a beating in the press, even facing calls for his resignation. More than a hundred men were working under him. Arrests were made daily of men said to be "annoying" little children on the street, but none could be connected to the killings. The *Evening World* put up a $2,000 reward; Police Commissioner Woods announced that members of the force were eligible to collect it.

City residents began to take matters into their own hands. On one occasion a patrolman had to draw his revolver to rescue Alfred Morane, accused of stabbing twelve-year-old Harry Re in the thigh as he was playing near his home. Instantly, swarms of men went after Morane, yelling, "He's a ripper!" On May 17, rumors spread that the New York Ripper was in custody; a thousand people congregated outside the police station. On May 19, more than fifty people kicked and beat a man they had somehow concluded was the Ripper; two cops had to beat their way through the crowd with nightsticks to rescue him as he lay on the sidewalk dripping with blood.

An *Evening World* reporter encountered Anna Selzan walking up and down the street in an attempt to entrap the Ripper, using young Margaret Berchers, a friend's daughter, as bait.

"You see," Selzan said, "I decided to capture the ripper myself, and the only way was through a decoy. Margaret, you see, walks up and down in front of the Murray and adjacent homes, loitering at the entrances of hallways when she can without attracting too much attention. I stay on this side of the street to give the alarm to rush over and grab the ripper when he seizes her. What do you think of my plan?"

After interviewing the little girl, the *World* reporter wrote, "Margaret did not think much of it when it was explained to her that the real Jack the Ripper killed little girls without ceremony, and Miss Selzan could not persuade her to resume the decoying job."

"Never mind," Miss Selzan told the reporters. "I look like a little girl myself. You will see me back in the morning, dressed in short skirts, with pigtails down my back. I can be my own decoy. I'll get the ripper yet."

Again, authorities weren't exactly reassuring.

"The situation is very serious in this city with this man at liberty," Coroner Israel Feinberg said. "If he is not caught within the next ten days, there will be another revolting murder at his hands. I advise all parents, especially in the East Side, to keep their children in after dark and not to let them play in the hallways."

And it wasn't just New York City. When rumors circulated that the Ripper was in the vicinity, fifty mothers rushed into a school in suburban White Plains demanding they be allowed to take their children home. In Montclair, New Jersey, about one hundred mothers stormed the Baldwin Street School, hysterical after rumors surfaced that the Ripper had been prowling about nearby. The same thing happened in Hoboken, New Jersey, following a rumor that the Ripper was in town, spread, newspapers reported, by a "demented" woman in black.

In the midst of this hysteria, two New York City girls—one ten and one twelve—thought it would be hilarious to send letters to two families threatening their children with kidnapping and murder. On May 12, a note from a person claiming to be the Ripper was traced to an eighteen-year-old woman annoyed by her employer over something and wanting to scare them.

Then came the letters to Mrs. Murray.

The first arrived on the afternoon of May 6 as Mrs. Murray sat weeping at the side of her son's coffin:

> Dear Mrs. Murray: I really feel sorry for you as I sit in my room here in this neighborhood and watch this crowd of police looking for me. But when their excitement cools off, immediately some evening after dinner I am going out and kill again. While I feel sorry for you, you must understand that I must see blood and cut flesh. These police can never get me. I have them guessing. Lovingly, R. F. C.

The letter, written in pencil, was enclosed in an envelope on the flap of which were the initials R. F. C. On the back the name R. F. Crane was crossed out.

On May 7, Mrs. Murray received another three letters: One, typed on a sheet of ruled paper, warned, "Your little girl will be killed in a few days if you do not call off the police. I remain, Jack the Ripper."

Another letter said, "I am the man who killed your boy. The police are a lot of boobs, and I am going to do it again. Signed, A. Rich."

In still another, the writer threatened, "I will do the same thing over again in the neighborhood of Fiftieth and Fifty-fourth Streets, between Fifth and Eleventh avenues."

Police dispatched a team of detectives to Midtown West, where they apprehended a man entering apartment hallways. Unable to speak English, he told police through an interpreter that he was a Greek actor presenting a Greek-language play that evening and, after worrying about it all night, was looking for the lead actress to offer her suggestions.

Faurot told reporters he believed the letters were the works of cranks.

Then, a month later and one hundred miles away, a man by the name of George Blumlein confessed to having killed both Leonore Cohn and Charles Murray, and then cutting out their livers.

## Philadelphia Story

On the afternoon of June 22, Philadelphia police noticed Blumlein pacing up and down the corridor outside headquarters. For hours. Finally, they stepped outside to ask him exactly what the hell he was doing.

"I came to see the man in charge, and I want to ask him something," Blumlein responded. "I want you to get me a warrant for a man in Greenwich Street, New York. He wants to cut my liver out."

Reaching into his pocket, Blumlein pulled out a pocketknife with a broken blade.

"Here," he said, "I've got something for you."

Blumlein, a thirty-year-old unemployed carpenter/painter, had lived with his common-law wife in a two-room flat on the fourth floor of a tenement on East Fifteenth Street in New York until two weeks earlier. He said he had brought three trunks with him to Philly, one containing seven canaries. His wife had just given birth, and once the baby was born, he gave away one bird and opened a window so that the others could fly off. His baby would be his new bird, he said.

Faurot hurried down to Philly to interrogate the suspect. Afterward, he told the press, "This man Blumlein is a study for psychologists and alienists. He appears to be the victim of recurring homicidal mania, the spells coming on every six or seven weeks, according to his wife. It is an interesting fact in this connection that six weeks elapsed between the murder of Leonore Cohn and Charlie."

Charles Murray's mother visited Blumlein's Manhattan tenement building to interview neighbors, but left convinced he wasn't responsible for her son's death. Blumlein eventually recanted his confession and was dispatched to a psychiatric hospital for observation. On July 12, he was released.

## The Meteorologist

On July 25, the *New-York Tribune* ran a story about Staten Island meteorologist Gerrard Hickson, who was convinced he had unmasked the Ripper. Hickson, eyeing the $2,000 reward, had given up his job to devote himself full-time to the manhunt.

"From the start, I was convinced that the police were not approaching the problem from the correct angle," Hickson said. "Scientific deduction and careful reasoning is the only way to work on such a case."

Hickson was convinced the Ripper was someone police themselves had earlier suspected. His wife wrote a letter to his suspect asking for a date. The man responded, enabling Hickson to compare his handwriting with that of the person who had penned the Jack the Ripper letters. A perfect match, he said.

"Why, even the police admitted it," he said. "And what do they do? Procrastinate! The other night they promised to arrest him. I hired two automobiles and a motion picture machine to photograph them as they brought him out of the house in shackles. What did they do? Backed down cold. And me having spent $25 for the outfit."

## "HELL HATH NO FURY"

On August 16, Baltimore police arrested Edgar Jones on a charge of defrauding a local boardinghouse owner—no huge deal until his boozed-up girlfriend, Grace Elliott, dropped a bombshell:

"Do you know you got the man here who has been hunted all over as the New York Ripper?" she said. "This has been worrying me for months. I am giving away the man I love. Jones is the man who, last spring, killed two children in New York. He killed the little Cohn girl and the little Murray boy. He is Jack the Ripper, and if you don't believe me, investigate my story."

Her story was that she and Jones, who police believed was actually Atilleo Fasco, were employed at Bellevue hospital the previous spring, Jones as an orderly and Elliott as a cook. On the night of March 10, she said, Jones came home with blood on his clothes. When Elliott asked for an explanation, he said he had murdered a little girl with his knife. The next day she read in the papers about the death of Leonore Cohn. On the night of May 3, she said, Jones again came home with bloodstains, this time confessing that he had killed a little boy.

"And I read about that Murray boy's death the next day, but still I didn't tell on my man, because I loved him," Elliott said.

Shortly afterward, she said, they moved to Baltimore. The knife Jones had used in the killings was already in police possession, having been confiscated on July 30 when Jones was arrested for drunk and disorderly conduct.

Interviewed again the next day—this time sober—Elliott stuck to her story.

"Look here," she said, "if you are a real copper you won't let that man Jones get away from you. He's the man who murdered two children in New York last spring."

The New York Police Department's Lieutenant Patrick Gildea headed down to Baltimore to investigate Elliott's accusations. Her dates, of course, were off: Cohn had been killed on March 19 and Murray on May 4. But Baltimore police confirmed Elliott's story about the knife. Police also checked with Bellevue, who told them a woman named Grace Jones had applied for work there the previous March and was directed to the Mills Training School for Nurses across the street, where she was hired as an assistant cook. When she mentioned to the school superintendent that her husband was looking for work too, he was brought on as a night watchman. Both had worked at the school until the second week of April. Several weeks later, they showed up again begging for money.

At first, Jones merely laughed when confronted with Elliott's accusations. He finally started to respond, but Baltimore detective Lieutenant Herman Pohler wasn't buying anything he had to say.

"You are lying to me," Pohler said. "Why do you do that? If you have nothing to conceal, why did you lie?"

"It's none of your business," Jones replied.

In the end, Elliott wound up recanting her accusations, and Gildea declared that Jones was no longer a suspect in the Ripper killings.

It would be another eighteen months before New York police announced another significant break in the case—or so they thought.

## False Alarm

On a cloudy winter morning in February 1917, eighteen-year-old Ruth Cruger left her home on Claremont Avenue in the Morningside Heights neighborhood of New York City to have her ice skates sharpened at the repair shop of Alfredo Cocchi on 127th Street. She never returned home.

The following morning, her older sister, Helen, stopped by Cocchi's shop to search for her missing sister but found the place shuttered. *Curious*, she thought. Later that morning, she returned. Still closed. Finally, at about 2:30 p.m., she found Cocchi hunched over a bicycle as several women waited to have their baby carriages repaired.

"Did my sister leave her skates to be sharpened yesterday?" Helen asked.

Yes, Cocchi replied, a young woman had indeed left a pair of skates to be sharpened in the morning and returned for them later in the day.

"What kind of skates were they?"

"They were fastened on shoes like you have on," Cocchi answered.

"Was she a dark and attractive girl?" Helen asked.

"Yes."

Helen reported the conversation to her dad, Henry, who phoned the police. Cocchi was a respectable businessman, a detective told him, but he agreed to pay him a visit to see if he knew anything about Ruth's disappearance. The detective later wrote up a one-line report: "I searched the cellar."

Two days after Ruth Cruger's disappearance, Alfredo Cocchi also vanished, leaving behind his wife and child. On May 31, he turned up in Italy, his native country.

The NYPD seemed content to drop the investigation, suspecting that Ruth might have been caught up in the growing epidemic of missing girls rumored to be sold into white slavery. But Henry Cruger hired a woman lawyer turned gumshoe, Grace Humiston, who would become internationally known after breaking the Cruger case wide open. When Humiston paid a visit to Cocchi's shop hoping to search the cellar herself, the missing repairman's wife, wielding a brick, sneered, "I'll split your skull with this brick if you try to come in here." Humiston shared the threat with Police Commissioner Arthur Woods, who secured a search warrant. Humiston herself, along with a friend of the Cruger family, found Ruth's body buried six feet beneath the cellar floor of Cocchi's shop on June 18. Cruger's skull had been crushed from behind, just above the left ear. A deep gash in her abdomen extended to her spine, carved with the blade of her skate. Largely on the strength of this case, Humiston became known as "Mrs. Sherlock Holmes."

Six days after Cruger's body was found, Faurot said the NYPD was investigating whether Cocchi was responsible for the deaths of Leonore Cohn and Charles Murray.

"These two persons and Ruth Cruger are the only persons killed by a 'ripper' in this city in recent years, and it seems strange that the three cases took place within a period of two years," Faurot said.

Dr. Carlos F. MacDonald, an alienist, concurred, which may be one reason why you don't see many alienists around anymore.

In the end, Cocchi was found guilty of Cruger's murder but cleared of any involvement in the slayings of Cohn and Murray. Humiston's allegations of NYPD negligence triggered an investigation revealing that motorcycle officers were sending speeding offenders to Cocchi so that he could fix their tickets for a small fee, most of which he kicked back to the officers.

## SOMETHING'S FISHY

Some online sleuths are keen on pinning the Cohn-Murray murders on a wack job named Hamilton Howard "Albert" Fish (aka the Gray man, the Werewolf of Wysteria, the Brooklyn Vampire, and the Moon Maniac), a rapist, child molester, and cannibal known to have slain at least three children between July 1924 and June 1928, but there's no evidence linking Fish to either of the crimes. Fish was finally apprehended on December 13, 1934; convicted of the murder and kidnapping of ten-year-old Grace Budd of Manhattan; and executed in the electric chair on January 16, 1936. The chief defense witness at Fish's trial was psychiatrist Fredric Wertham, best known as the author of the 1954 book *Seduction of the Innocent*, which argued, among other things, that comic books encouraged juvenile delinquency, Batman and Robin were gay, Wonder Woman was a lesbian, and Superman was fascistic. At Fish's trial, Wertham argued that the killer was obsessed with the biblical story of Abraham and Isaac and believed that sacrificing a boy would absolve him of his own sins, of which there were many. In arguing that Fish's life should be spared, Wertham told the court, "He is insane."

3

# Who Is Buried in Greenfield Cemetery?

## *Hempstead, Long Island*

On the morning of April 11, 1904, Benjamin Sprague and his friend Percy Van De Water were passing through the woods near Greenfield Cemetery outside of Hempstead, in Long Island, New York, when something caught the two boys' attention: a silhouette up ahead that looked like a woman, leaning against a chestnut tree with her head bent forward, obscuring her face. The boys avoided the figure; it seemed like maybe someone had too much to drink and went out to the woods to sleep it off. However, when they passed back that way several hours later, the woman was still there in the same position. The pair ran off seeking help, returning with John Hartman, a laborer who worked in the cemetery, where Benjamin's father was the caretaker, and Harry Gardiner, a marble worker from nearby Hempstead. As they approached, it soon became evident that the woman was neither intoxicated nor sleeping: She was dead and had been for some time.

### THE BODY OUTSIDE OF GREENFIELD CEMETERY

Gardiner alerted Nassau County district attorney James P. Niemann and acting coroner Archer B. Wallace, who both soon arrived at the scene. The dead woman appeared to be about thirty-five years old, with brown eyes and black hair, tinged with gray streaks. She was of average height and weight, and it appeared that she might have been dead for about a week. The body showed no immediate signs indicating the cause of death, although her lips were noticeably blackened as if they had been badly burned.

The heavy rains of the past few days had drenched her stylish clothes: She wore a shawl cape with a feathered edge over a much-worn black dress of woolen

Lynch crime scene
BROOKLYN EAGLE

material, and brown stockings, with accompanying black lace shoes, seemingly recently purchased. Her undergarments were white and made from quality materials. She also wore a plain, unadorned wedding band, and a silver locket hung from her neck. On her head was a large, flat black hat adorned with three feathers. Notably, any identifying labels or marks had been cut or torn from her clothes. Indeed, there was nothing on the woman or in the immediate vicinity to offer any direct clue as to her identity.

Fastened to the woman's waist was a chatelaine bag containing a string of beads, a rosary, a small cross, forty-seven cents, an assortment of toiletries, a number of printed prayers, and a note that read, "I am sick and can get no relief. I hope all will forgive me. I have struggled and struggled, I cannot close hardly an eye at night, so I see something, I don't know what. Good-by [*sic*], all my people, don't grieve after me. I am not worth it. Farewell." The note was written in ink on a plain piece of paper and was unsigned.

Investigators turned up a few other items near the body, but were unsure if they were relevant or had just been randomly lost there: a pocketknife and a rubber fountain pen encircled by two golden bands, one of which had the year "1903" engraved within, while the other had the initials "O.M." Most tellingly, on the ground near the body was a half empty two-ounce bottle containing carbolic acid, and a small wineglass. Although her identity remained elusive, the immediate facts strongly suggested a suicide.

On April 12, Dr. J. H. B. Denton of the coroner's office performed an autopsy with revealing results. The woman's lungs were ecchymosed—bruised, caused by the bursting of blood vessels—with a small amount of fluid in the lower cavity. Her heart was "flaccid," and there was a small clot in the left ventricle, while the right was filled with fluid. There was a bloody discharge emanating from the nose.

Her lips were badly seared and blackened, presumably from drinking the acid; however, defying expectations, Denton's examination found no evidence of any carbolic acid in the stomach. He did find a contusion that had badly swollen above her left eye, which had previously been hidden behind her hair. The eye was abraded, indicating it had received a blow, and there was evidence it had hemorrhaged. Lastly, the autopsy revealed that the dead woman had been in an advanced stage of pregnancy, or in the language of the day "in a delicate state."

## Who Is Martha Laimbeer?

Following the startling results of Denton's autopsy, authorities not only were left with the question of who the young dead woman was, but also needed to determine whether she had taken her own life or if the tragic scene outside Greenfield Cemetery had been carefully staged to conceal a murder. Efforts to track down where the pocketknife or pen had been purchased proved futile, and authorities were largely reliant on newspaper stories detailing the discovery of the body attracting the attention of someone who knew something and was willing to come forward.

Mary Peasell, mother of the undertaker who attended to the body, was certain she knew the dead woman. She had called on her at her home in Hempstead the week before, attempting to sell her some bric-a-brac or other. The woman had even left her contact information—Mrs. A. W. Daum, of Hempstead—in case Mrs. Peasell changed her mind and wanted to buy something. Coroner Wallace traveled to Hempstead with county detective Abram Furman to try to track the woman down. Although initially frustrated in their efforts, Furman found Mrs. Daum alive and well at Central Park near Island Trees on April 13.

Within a week of the story going public, at least a dozen people had visited the morgue thinking the dead woman might be a missing loved one. George Need of Brooklyn was looking for his wife, who had disappeared from their home two weeks earlier. Annie Cantwell from Manhattan thought it might be her missing sister. Another gentleman from Manhattan called looking for his daughter, Sara Harris, an actress who sometimes went by the stage name Selma; it later emerged she had accepted a week's engagement for a play in Memphis, Tennessee. Time and time again family members left the morgue despondently, shaking their heads no, unable to confirm the identity of the mysterious corpse.

On April 14, Dr. Denton received an anonymous letter from someone claiming to be a friend of the dead woman's family that read, "Dear sir—In the name of charity, in the name of your noble profession and of the distracted relatives who shun public disgrace, I beg of you to spare the poor woman suicide from a pauper's grave. Please give her a decent burial with the $100 enclosed. Purchase a grave and a coffin and retain sufficient to repay you for your trouble. . . . Bury her under the name of Martha Laimbeer. Body will be claimed in the future. Please don't publish this letter. The poor woman had often threatened to kill herself. God will reward you for your kindness."

And so, the woman was buried in Greenfield Cemetery on April 19, close to where her body was found, under the name Martha Laimbeer. The burial was delayed while officials argued over regulations dictating where nonresidents were allowed to be buried, but when it finally commenced, hundreds of curious onlookers gathered around the grave while local resident George Wallace said a short prayer. Coroner Wallace cited her cause of death as unknown, and it seemed like the mystery would endure, as developments in the case went dormant.

## A Case of Murder?

After several months of no news, "Martha Laimbeer" abruptly returned to the headlines in early September as reports surfaced that self-proclaimed criminologist William Clemens had solved the case and would reveal all imminently. Clemens was a notorious publicity hound, who had promoted himself as "America's Sherlock Holmes," and also somewhat of a charlatan—he often claimed to be Mark Twain's cousin, which Twain adamantly denied. Clemens had a history of barnstorming a town when a high-profile mystery emerged, inveigling himself with authorities to get access and inside information, only to use it to his own advantage, promoting outrageous, unsubstantiated theories almost as facts; however, he also had a knack for digging up dirt that others missed.[1]

On September 11, Coroner Wallace announced plans to resume the inquest; he elaborated that he had never believed the woman had committed suicide, and a letter he received from Clemens, who had been covertly looking into the case since its early days, had reinforced his belief that the girl had been murdered and promised that her killer would soon be captured. Wallace shared portions of the letter that the infamous criminologist had sent to him with reporters, to include a description of the killer: He had a light complexion, with blue eyes and brown hair, and lived in Brooklyn.

Clemens later elaborated, "I am fully satisfied that the woman was murdered in her own home, and that her body was then dragged or carried through the woods to Greenfield Cemetery, two days after her death. Her death, I have established, was caused by shock, following a blow dealt her in the temple, and just over her eye with some heavy block of wood or iron."

As the continuation of the inquest neared, expectations had shifted from suicide, and it was thought that Clemens would appear with corroborating witnesses explaining how the girl had been murdered. Instead, the resumed session included only testimony from Dr. Denton, who had performed the autopsy, and Dr. Walter Kent, an expert in chemicals. After Denton initially proclaimed there was no trace of carbolic acid in the woman's stomach, DA Niemann had brought in Kent to run some follow-up tests. Kent testified that he had the contents of the stomach tested through six different analyses, finding traces of carbolic acid each time. Denton's initial findings of no acid in the stomach, which had helped spark the belief that it was a case of murder, had been erroneous. Although Clemens and his promised revelations didn't make an appearance, Wallace said they would be coming shortly.

## Who Is Margaret Lynch?

On the evening of September 19, DA Niemann issued a bombshell statement to the press that the woman buried under the name Martha Laimbeer had been identified as Miss Margaret Lynch, daughter of a well-known contractor in Brooklyn. Soon after, Father Peter J. Burns of St. John the Baptist in Brooklyn emerged, claiming to be a family friend and spokesperson for the Lynches. He had known Margaret Lynch—"Mattie" to family and friends—since she was

---

1. For further adventures featuring the infamous Will Clemens, seek out *Murder at Teal's Pond: Hazel Drew and the Mystery That Inspired Twin Peaks*, by these same authors.

little. Father Burns said there was no question in his mind or in the minds of her family that the girl buried in Greenfield Cemetery was Margaret Lynch and that, furthermore, she had taken her own life. He offered as proof a letter given to him by Margaret's mother, Catherine Lynch, which her daughter had sent to her, describing Margaret's overwhelming unhappiness and intention to kill herself. Father Burns then shared Margaret's sad tale.

A little more than two years earlier, Margaret had become engaged to a young man named Oswald Maune—he had gifted her the pen bearing his initials, O. M., that was found near her body—a fellow parishioner in Father Burns's church. The Maunes and the Lynches were neighbors and had been friendly over the years, even vacationing together in the Catskills. However, soon

EVENING WORLD

after the engagement, Oswald began exhibiting increasingly erratic behavior that was exacerbated by his alcohol abuse: He was often found staggering on the streets, speaking nonsense in a manic state. His outbursts became so unpredictable that Margaret decided she would only see him at the Maunes' house, for fear of reproach from her stern father. During this time, while Oswald's mental health continued to decline, Margaret grew closer to the Maunes, who became a sort of second family. Before long, Oswald's condition became so severe that he was sent to the Kings Park asylum in Long Island—he was never released.

The whole affair triggered Margaret's own struggles with depression, which her family contended ultimately led to her tragic demise outside Greenfield Cemetery. The family had believed for some time that the dead girl was Margaret but wanted to avoid the publicity that coming forward would bring; they only did so now to quell the statements made by Wallace and the rumblings in the press by Clemens and others suggesting it had been a case of murder rather than suicide.

Despite these startling public admissions by Father Burns, authorities remained skeptical that the woman they buried was Margaret Lynch. Dr. John F. Shea, Margaret's dentist, was located, and he described the details of the work he had done on the dead girl, including many gold and silver fillings; Dr. Denton didn't recall seeing any such fillings during the autopsy. Also, the woman found near the cemetery was in her mid-thirties, while early reports said Margaret was a teenager (although this was later corrected by her family). Additionally, Coroner Archer Wallace had long been a proponent of the murder theory—perhaps influenced by the beliefs of Dr. Denton, who initially found no carbolic acid in her stomach and claimed the head wound would have been sufficient to cause death—and was resistant to change his views. Dr. Denton also happened to be Wallace's father-in-law.

DA Niemann was more open-minded about Father Burns's claims but needed more to go on than the ardent beliefs of the Lynch family. On the afternoon of September 27, Niemann had the body of the woman buried under the name of Martha Laimbeer exhumed. He had initially intended to have Dr. Shea serve as the primary identifier because of the extensive work the doctor had done on her teeth, thinking to spare the Lynch family the horror of seeing the now-decaying corpse. Regardless of the DA's concern, Margaret's mother and two of her sisters arrived at the cemetery and were ushered to the graveside, where a mob of press and curious onlookers had gathered. Notably, Coroner Wallace was absent during the exhumation, in St. Louis on vacation at the time.

Also absent that afternoon was Margaret's father, whom the rest of the family had kept in the dark as best they could—he only learned of the family's belief that Margaret was the Greenfield Cemetery corpse shortly before they contacted the authorities, having been told she was visiting relatives in Kansas. The family feared that if her father knew the truth, his violent nature might be roused.

There was a heavy, tense atmosphere as the simple coffin was lifted from the ground; the corpse's clothing, having been removed and stored at the time of burial, had already been viewed and identified by the family. As soon as the coffin was opened, the family, all dressed in black and wearing veils, immediately recognized the girl's face; although decomposition had set in, her general features were not greatly marred. Her hair also had streaks of gray, matching those that had developed in Margaret's hair during the trials of the past few years.

Margaret's sister, also named Catherine, gave a pitiful shriek and immediately burst into tears. In her anguish, she lost her footing and almost fell into the grave, save for the quick reflexes of her fiancé, who was able to catch her; she later fainted. Her mother dropped to her knees, sobbed, and moaned, "Mattie, my dear Mattie, my poor Mattie girl!" She tenderly laid her hand on the brow of the girl, saying a fervent prayer. As she leaned forward, as if to kiss the girl, she was pulled back and led away. Margaret's sister Mary was more subdued, kneeling before the body, quietly praying.

Beyond the immediate recognition of their loved one, the Lynch women also all identified the silver medallion that still hung around the girl's neck as a Holy Agony medal; her sister Catherine had given it to her back in February after Margaret had told her she was pregnant—she had worn it ever since.

Dr. Shea was also at the grave and told Niemann that he could see that it was Margaret Lynch, whom he had known for the past nine years, and didn't need to examine her teeth. The DA insisted that he proceed, and Shea found the silver and gold linings as he expected, but curiously, she was missing a gold cap. Later, at the inquest, her sister Mary revealed the cap had fallen out at some point.

With the identity of the dead woman seemingly confirmed at long last, the details of the events leading up to Margaret's demise started to come out through the press and ultimately at the inquest, where her mother and sisters were called upon to testify: The Lynch family was unanimous in blaming one man for Margaret's tragic end.

## THE TRAGIC DETAILS

Margaret was understandably in dismay after the institutionalization of her fiancé, and seemed to find some solace in spending time with her former betrothed's family. Oswald Maune Sr. was a prominent printer; he and his wife, Alice, were in their late fifties and had two other sons, one of whom was a Catholic priest. In the summer of 1903, Margaret accompanied the Maunes on a trip to Freeport, Long Island, spending a month at the Woodcleft Inn, not far from Greenfield Cemetery, where the body was found.

At the inquest, Harry Van Riper, the manager of the Woodcleft Inn, was called to give evidence about the Maunes' visit with Margaret Lynch, who had registered at the hotel as the Maunes' niece. Van Riper was a reluctant witness but eventually revealed enough to paint a telling picture.

Oswald Sr. had arrived with only his "niece" initially, with Alice joining them after some time. Margaret stayed in an adjoining room to the Maunes at the rear of the hotel's second floor. During their stay, Margaret would frequently go on long walks or bike rides, often joined by Oswald. Van Riper elaborated that the pair were practically inseparable, while Mrs. Maune would usually be found alone on the front porch reading her Bible. The innkeeper went on to describe Margaret and Oswald as being "very friendly," and although he hadn't witnessed it firsthand, other guests had told him there was tension between the Maunes because of his relationship with Margaret.

On August 10, Alice had had enough and was in such a hurry to depart that she had to borrow money from the hotel to pay for transportation home. Although the Maunes had been booked to stay until September 15, Oswald and Margaret also checked out the next day. When Margaret returned home, her spirits were not improved and seemed to worsen over the following weeks and months. In February 1904, six months after leaving the Woodcleft Inn, she revealed to her family that she was pregnant. Soon after, she moved out of the family home, her location unknown for some time, until she finally contacted her mother and sisters from Mrs. Freedman's boardinghouse on Lenox Avenue.

Her sisters, Catherine and Mary, came to visit her at Freedman's and found her in a sad, sorry state. Almost immediately after their arrival, Margaret abruptly left the apartment, only to return soon after accompanied by Oswald Maune Sr. In front of her sisters, she accused Maune of being the man responsible for her condition. He did not deny the accusation, although he cryptically added, "I am not the only one who is leading a double life." He promised he would do all he could to support Margaret, and in early April, he escorted her by carriage to the Sisters of Charity maternity hospital in Manhattan, where she was admitted under the alias of Margaret Lawrence.

Margaret's depression and anxiety continued under the care of the sisters, and her behavior grew erratic. One night, she escaped from the hospital and was found wandering around Central Park with a loaded revolver; she broke down crying as a police officer took the gun from her, and bemoaned that she didn't have the strength to end her life. On April 5, Margaret called her sister Catherine, saying she was planning on going away for a week or more and that she shouldn't try to call her or write to her at the hospital until she had first heard from her—this was the last contact the family would have with Margaret. Shortly thereafter, she snuck out of the Sisters of Charity again, this time never to return.

Although the Lynch family revealed that Oswald Maune Sr. was the one who had sent the note with the hundred-dollar bill to pay for her grave—using the false name Martha Laimbeer, whose initials were identical to Margaret's—they were adamant that he was also the villain behind their beloved Mattie taking her own life. Through tears, her sisters and mother testified at the inquest as to how distressed she was and that she had frequently threatened suicide. According to her sister Mary, Margaret had said of Maune Sr., "He has driven me to a suicide's grave." And yet Maune was never questioned at the inquest, despite rumors that he would be called to appear; apparently his request to communicate with authorities through his lawyer was granted. In the end, despite being morally responsible, he bore no legal culpability for Margaret's suicide. And so, it seemed the mystery of the unknown woman found near Greenfield Cemetery had come to a conclusion.

## Final Twist

However, in November 1905, more than a year after the inquest ended, the case took a final bizarre turn when Coroner Wallace issued his final ruling: "From the testimony taken before me, I conclude that the deceased came to her death by foul means, and that her body was brought to the place where found, at least one or two days after death. Her name I do not know, but it was probably Margaret Lehmaier. I am satisfied that the deceased was not Margaret Lynch, and believe that Margaret Lynch was alive several weeks after the body of the deceased was found. No conclusive evidence of the death of Margaret Lynch has yet been given, and for aught I know she may yet be living." Wallace acknowledged that the carbolic acid found in her stomach was the cause of death, but firmly believed it was forced upon her by an assailant, possibly after she had already been rendered unconscious.

Notably, the name Margaret Lehmaier had never previously been mentioned over the course of the investigation, and Wallace made no attempt to explain who she was in his statement. Was he perhaps confusing her with

Martha Laimbeer, the name cited in the anonymous letter received by Dr. Denton (eventually determined to have been written by Oswald Maune Sr.)? There's no evidence that anyone named Martha Laimbeer even really existed. Or had Wallace found a brand-new suspect in trying to identify the Greenfield Cemetery corpse? If so, he never explained further.

James Niemann was no longer the district attorney, but upon hearing of Wallace's decision, he responded, "From all the facts obtained by my investigation, which I consider was thorough, the testimony given before Justice Wallace and the identification of the Lynch girl's body by her family, I cannot see any substantial ground for a decision that foul play caused death, or a supposition that the body was not that of Margaret Lynch."

Niemann pointed to the overwhelming amount of evidence supporting his argument: the handwriting of the suicide note found with the body matching samples of Margaret's; the pen from her former fiancé with the "O.M." inscription; the note sent to her mother saying she intended suicide; the admitted culpability of Oswald Maune Sr.; and the obviously authentic identification of the body by the family and Dr. Shea after the exhumation at Greenfield Cemetery (which Wallace had missed, on vacation in St. Louis at the time). And yet as far as the official record of Nassau County is concerned, Margaret Lynch went missing and never returned home, while the body of the woman found near Greenfield Cemetery and buried under the name Martha Laimbeer technically remains unidentified. R.I.P.

4

# A Lady Vanishes

## *New York City*

Nobody has ever been able to figure out what happened to Dorothy Harriet Camilla Arnold, the United States's oldest unsolved missing person's case. On a blistering cold afternoon in December 1910, Dorothy was out shopping for a party dress in downtown Manhattan when she ran into Gladys King, a friend from college. Dorothy was coming out of Brentano's bookstore, having purchased a collection of romantic short stories. The two girls chatted amiably, light talk about what they wanted for Christmas and an upcoming party that Dorothy was hosting. They parted in good humor; Gladys actually had her RSVP for the party on her, and they joked about saving on the postage as Dorothy took it from her right there on the street.

After this brief encounter, amid the hustle and bustle of the hectic New York City landscape, Dorothy seemingly vanished off the face of the earth. And ever since, no one has been able to figure out why.

### DOROTHY

Dorothy was young, beautiful, well-liked, and wealthy. But there was more to her than the superficial life of an NYC socialite. She was described by friends and family as "mentally brilliant." In 1905, she earned a degree in literature from prestigious Bryn Mawr University, one of the Seven Sisters, the traditional women's colleges that served as counterparts to the Ivy League schools. Upon graduation, she had intended to pursue a career as an author; she regularly submitted short stories and poetry to various magazines and journals.

Dorothy Arnold
LIBRARY OF CONGRESS

Dorothy had loving parents, whom she lived with along with her younger siblings, Hinckley and Marjorie; her older brother, John, had moved out by 1910. By all accounts, the Arnolds were a close-knit family. They were all intimately involved with the extensive manhunt that followed her disappearance, and the unanswered questions surrounding the case haunted each of them to their graves.

Dorothy's father, Francis R. Arnold, was a successful importer of perfumes and other fine goods who could trace his roots back to the crossing of the *Mayflower*. Mary Arnold, his wife, had roots in Canada, from where her parents had emigrated. The Arnolds were well-to-do and prominent in society circles; Francis's brother-in-law had been a justice on the US Supreme Court. The Arnolds were reported to be millionaires in 1910, although they would end up spending a good portion of their fortune in an extensive, worldwide search for their missing daughter.

Besides her immediate family, Dorothy had a wide network of friends—mostly girls her age whom she knew from her time at Bryn Mawr, located outside Philadelphia. While a student there, she met young women from Philadelphia, New York City, Boston, Washington, DC, and elsewhere. And Dorothy seemed to keep up with and visit them all. Josephine Bates, a friend from Bryn Mawr, said, "Dorothy was one of the most popular girls in the class, lighthearted, talented, and congenial. It will break the hearts of the girls if she is lost for all time, as she was a favorite."

Her father added, "My daughter was of an independent nature—not stubborn or perverse or even self-willed, but high spirited and full of initiative, and it is quite true that she was ambitious to really do something for herself." Others who knew her described her as "pretty, aristocratic, refined, ideally happy in her home, devoted to her parents, without any serious love affair of any sort, content, absolutely normal and balanced in her thoughts and her life."

Beyond engaging in the social activities seemingly mandated of the upper class during this period, Dorothy did not seem one to take her advantageous position in society for granted. She was always reading and enjoyed going to museums and the theater. Most of all, Dorothy was passionate about literature and aspired to be a great writer. She had submitted poetry and short stories to magazines like *Cosmopolitan* but received only rejection letters for her efforts.

In most missing persons cases or unsolved murders, investigators look for potential suspects from a victim's past romantic entanglements. Police and private investigators talked to Dorothy's family and friends to see if there was some close intimate who could have been involved in her disappearance. Initial reports indicated that Dorothy didn't really have a long list of past boyfriends; there had been a few young men who had come to her home to court her, in the practice of the day, but nothing serious had developed. After Dorothy vanished, all the young men whom she had been involved with at some point were placed under surveillance and subsequently interviewed. Investigators and family members absolved these men of having anything to do with Dorothy's disappearance.

However, as the investigation wore on, it would be learned that one of these gentlemen may have had a larger place in Dorothy's heart than the others. And this gentleman was not in New York City, but somewhere overseas.

## THE DISAPPEARANCE

Late on the morning of December 12, 1910, Dorothy was planning to head downtown to buy an evening gown for her sister Marjorie's coming-out party. Marjorie was turning eighteen, and Dorothy was hosting the party at her parents' home. Invitations had already gone out to sixty of her friends and classmates from Bryn Mawr, and musicians had been engaged to perform. As Dorothy prepared to leave, her mother offered to accompany her, but perhaps mindful of the cold weather, Dorothy insisted that she needn't bother—she might not even find anything suitable, and if she did and needed assistance, she would call. She kissed her mother goodbye and headed out the door around 11:30 a.m.

A half hour later, Dorothy was shopping, but not yet for a gown. She stopped at Park & Tilford's on Fifth Avenue, near Fifty-ninth Street, where she purchased a half pound of chocolate. The salesclerks there distinctly remembered Dorothy, and the receipt, charged to her father's account, confirmed she had been there at noon. An hour later, she was in Brentano's bookstore farther up Fifth Avenue, near Twenty-seventh Street, where she bought *An Engaged Girl's Sketches*, a collection of light short stories by Emily Calvin Blake. On her way out of the store, she bumped into her college chum; they chatted for some time before Dorothy accepted her RSVP with a laugh as her friend departed, having plans for lunch with her mother. The investigation would turn up witnesses, of varying degrees of credibility, who would also place her at the post office or, later in the day, at a steamboat ticket agency. Nonetheless, the brief chat with her friend outside the bookstore is the last confirmed sighting of Dorothy Arnold.

## THE HUNT

Dorothy's family was alerted to her disappearance almost immediately. As noted, the Arnolds were a tight family, and Dorothy's failure to appear at dinner without calling her parents beforehand instantly told them something was off. As the hours ticked by, their apprehension grew, and finally they summoned John S. Keith, the family's personal lawyer and friend, for advice. Keith was a junior partner at Gavin & Armstrong, and soon the entire firm was involved in an ever-expanding investigation. Keith would continue to play a prominent role in the search for Dorothy, often acting as a mouthpiece, and sometimes shield, for the Arnold family when dealing with the press.

Consulting with Keith and his firm's partners, the Arnolds made the crucial decision early on not to reveal Dorothy's disappearance to the public. Indeed, while a swarm of private detectives almost immediately embarked on a worldwide search for Dorothy, even the New York City Police were not alerted until two weeks after she went missing. The motive for the Arnolds' decision to hold their cards so close to their chest was not malicious. Rather, they had known of other similar instances where rich young society women had mysteriously "vanished" only to turn up later, having run away from their parents as an act of rebellion or because of a romantic liaison—such circumstances could lead to scandal and public scorn for both the family and the woman herself. As the Arnolds initially believed and hoped that Dorothy would return home unharmed, they chose to withhold all information from the public for six weeks. This delay may have been a pivotal misstep in determining Dorothy's fate.

Despite this gaffe, easily recognizable with hindsight, Francis Arnold and his family appeared to do everything else in their not inconsiderable power to locate Dorothy; this included spending thousands and thousands of dollars tracking down clues and tips. After they conferred with Keith and others close to the family, little time was wasted in organizing an extensive global search. Although the police were not informed initially, a small army of private investigators, including members of the notorious Pinkerton agency, was soon deployed to determine Dorothy's whereabouts, scouring New York City and beyond.

Neighborhoods were canvassed. Morgues, asylums, hotels, and boardinghouses were visited and revisited. Detectives went from bed to bed in public hospitals. They spoke to her vast circle of friends; no one could shed any light on Dorothy's disappearance. When all of these efforts failed to yield any clue of real value, the detectives fanned out to neighboring cities: Philadelphia, Boston, and Washington, DC, places where Dorothy had family and friends and visited often. Again, no trace of the missing woman. Nobody had seen anything; nobody knew anything.

Once the story had gone public, hundreds of tips, clues, and reported sightings of Dorothy flowed in: A rigger had spotted her in Hoboken, New Jersey, talking to two men before boarding a steamship heading overseas; two taxi drivers were overheard talking about Dorothy being held for ransom in Philadelphia; Dorothy was seen in Highland Falls wandering around the village with a gentleman, stopping to watch children ice-skate; in Chicago, a South Side woman swore that Dorothy had been to her home trying to sell her shoe polish.

Phone calls and letters poured into the Arnold home from people claiming they were holding Dorothy ransom or knew who was. At the height of the investigation, Mr. Arnold reported that in the previous three days, his daughter had been sighted on a train in Albany; in at least four different locations in Philadelphia; once each in Brooklyn, Flushing, Huntington, Long Island, and Norfolk, Virginia; and in a dozen separate instances in Manhattan. It was all a bit overwhelming. Still, the family's fortune allowed them to follow up each and every lead, no matter how far-fetched. Perhaps predictably at this point, despite the choking smoke, there was not any fire.

The investigators had determined that Dorothy's last known actions on December 12 had been to purchase a collection of light short stories and a half pound of chocolate. Could Dorothy have been preparing to pass the time on a long train trip? Detectives spoke with hundreds of railway ticket sellers, train conductors, and car porters; they also investigated ferryboats, outgoing trains, and all roads leading out of the city. There were a multitude of tips and alleged sightings; each lead was followed up on, and time and time again nothing helpful was uncovered.

A search of the contents of her room at her parents' house was fairly mundane and unremarkable but did yield two possible clues. Firstly, burned pieces of paper were discovered in her wastebasket. Although these remnants were eviscerated beyond discernment, the prevalent theory was that they may have been manuscripts that Dorothy had submitted to publishers who had subsequently rejected and returned them; it was speculated that she then destroyed them in her despair. Writing was important to Dorothy, and since graduating from Bryn Mawr five years earlier, she had failed to launch any sort of literary career, receiving rejection after rejection. Was her anguish so great that she considered taking her own life?

Dorothy had saved numerous pieces of correspondence, found bundled in her private desk. Many of these were from her friends from college, but a handful had been sent by young men who were known to have called upon Dorothy or had flowers sent to her. Even though her relationships with these young men may have had the air of romance, nothing in the letters revealed any sort of motivation connected to Dorothy's disappearance, or even exhibited signs of a more intimate nature. Three of the gentlemen lived in New York, and the family's detectives spent time surveilling each of the men before questioning them. Again, no sign of a serious romance or any reason to think they were connected to her disappearance.

## GEORGE GRISCOM JR. (AKA "JR.")

In keeping with the family's practice of avoiding scandal whenever possible, the names of these three young men were never revealed. However, a fourth man, determined to be living overseas at the time, would end up in the spotlight as the press finally joined the private detectives and police in looking for a solution to Dorothy's disappearance when the case went public in late January 1911. This fourth man's name was George Griscom Jr., known to his family and friends simply as "Jr." Jr. was the son of Elizabeth and George Griscom Sr., a Pittsburgh lawyer whom Jr. had worked for before his father's retirement. The younger Griscom was forty-two years old and still lived with his parents, splitting the time between their homes in Pittsburg and Florence, Italy.

Jr. had first become acquainted with Dorothy while vacationing in Nantucket, Massachusetts, in the summer of 1908. The pair continued to see each other, albeit sporadically, over the next couple of years. They also wrote to each other regularly; it was reported that her affection for Griscom grew over time.

Griscom once called upon Dorothy and the Arnolds at their summer home in York Harbor, Maine. Mr. Arnold came away from that encounter less than impressed with Jr., objecting to "any man that had no business." A family friend confirmed that Dorothy and her father had argued over Griscom, but added she thought that the dispute had been resolved. Francis later clarified that there was no ill will toward Jr., and rumors that he wouldn't allow him in his home were untrue; he added that he barely knew the man, only from their encounter at York Harbor.

GEORGE C. GRISCOM, JR.

NEWSPAPERS.COM

On September 19, a few months before her disappearance, while Dorothy had been vacationing with her family at their summer home in Nantucket, she departed alone, supposedly traveling to Boston to spend time with Theodora Bates, one of her Bryn Mawr chums who lived in Cambridge. In reality, Dorothy lied to her parents in order to meet up with Griscom in secret. Jr. had arrived in Boston on September 16 and engaged a room in a separate hotel in which Dorothy would stay.

Shortly after she arrived, Dorothy pawned approximately $500 (roughly $16,000 in today's dollars) of jewelry, receiving only $60 back (roughly $2,000 in today's dollars). She had to fund her clandestine getaway; Jr. had booked her a hotel room but left her to pay the bill. Reports about what the couple got up to were vague, but a friend of Dorothy's said they went to a country club for dinner a few nights and that Dorothy didn't spend the whole time in Jr.'s company. She ended up spending nearly a week in Boston before returning to Nantucket on September 25.

The correspondence from Jr. that investigators found in Dorothy's desk was deemed relatively harmless. Lorenzo Armstrong, one of the Arnolds' lawyers, said the letters from Griscom were "of a friendly nature, as a friend would write to another friend"; this did not appear to be the kind of obsessive love affair that could have fueled a crime of passion. Additionally, Griscom had a nearly incontrovertible alibi—he was in Florence when Dorothy disappeared, having sailed with his parents on November 5, more than a month before she had vanished.

Nevertheless, the Arnolds' investigation was extremely thorough, and Mr. Arnold's financial resources were considerable. After a series of back-and-forth wireless telegrams confirming the Griscoms were in Italy, Pinkerton detectives were deployed to Florence to track Jr. down and determine if he had any insight into Dorothy's whereabouts. Upon confirming his location, the detectives placed him under surveillance for some time and, after noticing nothing unusual in his actions, directly approached him about Dorothy. Jr.'s reaction of surprise and concern seemed genuine, and he answered the questions posed to him satisfactorily—apparently, this was another dead end.

However, weeks later, with other leads and clues leading nowhere, there was renewed interest in Griscom following the discovery of additional letters he had written to Dorothy. Although the content of these new finds was said to be as innocuous as previous correspondence, these new letters differed in that they were sent to the general delivery window at the post office—Dorothy had a secret account there, apparently for any correspondence she didn't want her family to know about.

Despite her father's objections after his initial encounter with Griscom in Maine, Dorothy had continued to see and speak to Jr. in secret, and an account at the general delivery window was the perfect way to hide their relationship. The Arnolds admitted that Dorothy had received two general delivery letters from Griscom but claimed her account at the post office was primarily used to correspond with publishers that she had been submitting manuscripts to. She had faced rejection more than once and had been teased by her brother John about her foundering writing career.

The Arnolds had discovered, in addition to the general delivery letters from Griscom, a bundle of roughly half a dozen steamship schedules among her possessions, suggesting thoughts of overseas travel. As such, while other leads had run dry, there was renewed interest among some of the Arnolds, particularly her mother, Mary, into what insight Griscom had into Dorothy's affairs. Even if Jr. wasn't responsible for her disappearance, could he know some secret of Dorothy's that might inform them of what had happened to her?

## European Escapade

On January 5, 1911, Mary Arnold and her oldest son, John, set sail for Florence on the steamship liner *La Lorraine*, having purchased last-minute tickets. They arrived in Florence nearly two weeks later, on January 18, and immediately set off to the Anglo-American Hotel where the Griscoms were staying. The Arnolds first tracked down Griscom Sr., explaining why they were there; the elder Griscom facilitated a meeting with the Arnolds and his son, which happened later in Jr.'s room.

Mary Arnold, wearing a veil in an attempt to stay out of the press, took the lead in demanding that Jr. turn over all correspondence he had from Dorothy immediately; Jr. was flustered. Not pleased with Jr.'s delay in complying with the request, John took over from his mother, more aggressively demanding answers. As the encounter intensified, one particular response from Jr. set John off, and he sprang up from his chair, striking Griscom violently. A second blow sent Jr. sprawling to the floor, and John leaped atop of him, slapping him repeatedly in the face while screaming, "Now give up the letter from sister!" At this point, a discombobulated Griscom unconsciously made a move for his pocket. Picking up on the gesture, John reached into the pocket and seized the concealed letter that had been sent by Dorothy.

After the drama died down, the letter was read, and like all previously reviewed correspondence, it was basically harmless and offered no clue as to what had happened to Dorothy. John once again called on the elder Griscom, explaining what had happened and apologizing for his actions. The senior Griscom was much agitated by the whole affair but accepted John's apology, and the two parted on good terms. After his encounter with the Griscoms, John returned home to NYC; his mother stayed behind in Europe with family friends, possibly continuing to search for traces of Dorothy.

While his wife and oldest son were on their European adventure, Francis Arnold and his advisers had finally made the decision to reveal Dorothy's disappearance to the public—reportedly, a family friend had confided in Francis that he had faced a similar situation a few years earlier; his missing daughter had never surfaced, and he had come to regret not making the affair public. As such, when returning from Italy, Dorothy's brother John was caught completely off-guard during a stopover in Gibraltar as reporters ambushed him with a barrage of questions about his reasons for traveling abroad. John's awkward responses were flustered and inconsistent: He said he had only just heard of Dorothy's disappearance from a cable received from his father and knew scant details. He claimed to have practically jumped on the first available steamer heading to the States, barely having time to pack a single bag of luggage. Why had he gone to Italy? Merely a business trip; he was there signing a contract for a proprietary article. He said he had sailed for Europe on January 3. No wait, it was actually December 3. As far as he knew, his mother was home in New York. The press instantly sensed something was off. What was John not telling them? Was Dorothy in Florence with her mother?

The story about John's trip to Florence would continue to shift until the truth at last came out. Family spokesperson Keith explained that because John didn't know the story had gone public, he wasn't sure what he should say when he was interrogated in Gibraltar. The press had no problem buying that story. Keith elaborated that John had been overseas strictly on business . . . initially. He had been to Paris and a few coastal cities in France, but thought there would be no harm in checking in on Jr. while he was in the area. No, his mother was certainly not with him; he had traveled alone; Mrs. Arnold was recuperating from the whole ordeal with friends. Keith was unwilling to disclose her location.

## Secrets

This lack of candor with the press and the public was not unique in terms of how the Arnolds handled the investigation. From the outset, they had withheld Dorothy's vanishing from the police for two weeks, and from the press and public for another month. The family was always guarded and protective of everyone within their circle; until Griscom was tracked down by the press, none of Dorothy's male admirers' names had been made public, and the identities of those who lived in New York were never revealed.

The Arnolds were perhaps most guarded when it came to their daughter's privacy. Initially, they claimed Dorothy had not been involved in any sort of romantic relationships, which was proven to be far from the truth. When it was revealed that letters from young gentlemen were found in her bedroom, the Arnolds downplayed them all as mere friendships. Clearly, at least regarding George Griscom Jr.—whom the press would uncover had an escapade with Dorothy in Boston—this was not the case. Any possible clue that involved Dorothy's personal life seemed to originate from newspapermen digging around rather than from the family or their lawyers.

It was the press that uncovered the letters Dorothy received from the general delivery window at the post office; they also exposed the details behind her relationship with Griscom, including her father's negative opinion of the man. Reporters would also learn that a few months before she vanished, Dorothy had asked her father if he would pay for an apartment of her own in Greenwich Village so that she could focus on her writing career; Francis, reflecting the pragmatic parental perspective that has endured for generations, was hardly swayed by her request, responding that she could write just as well at home as she could in an apartment. These family tiffs and messy romantic entanglements were the kinds of potentially embarrassing personal details the Arnolds were trying to keep out of the papers. Rightly or wrongly, they felt they could delineate what might be relevant to Dorothy's disappearance and didn't feel compelled to discuss anything beyond that line.

An unfortunate side effect of the family's secretive disposition was a belief, at times, by both the press and the police, that the Arnolds might be holding back some critical piece of information. Some newspapers speculated that Dorothy was not only alive and well, but that certain members of her family knew where she was or had even seen her. New York City Police deputy commissioner William J. Flynn, head of the official investigation into the disappearance, frequently stated that he believed she was alive and would return home soon; these assertions were made despite her immediate family—who all played an active role in investigating Dorothy's whereabouts—consistently maintaining they had not seen or heard from her since December 12. Francis Arnold, in particular, hardly ever wavered from his belief that Dorothy was deceased, likely assaulted while walking through Central Park, as she was prone to do. In retrospect, the family's half-truths and coyness with the surrounding facts of the case, although possibly well-intentioned, might have helped fuel public interest, creating the very sort of scandalous headlines they were hoping to avoid.

## JR. STATESIDE

And so, when the Griscoms returned from Florence in early February, they found themselves in the midst of a circus-like atmosphere fostered by the daily titillating headlines in the papers. Jr. and his parents packed up and sailed for home on the liner *Berlin* within a few days of their encounter with the Griscoms. And much like Dorothy's brother John, the Griscoms were ambushed at the stopover in Gibraltar by a horde of reporters in a frenzied search for a story.

Jr. was said to be amiable, but decidedly reticent to say much: He flatly refused to discuss Dorothy. Jr.'s parents were even more unsettled at suddenly being thrust into the scandalous spotlight. Reporters found the elder Griscom nervously pacing about the promenade, declining to answer questions; he rapidly fled belowdecks to the sanctuary of his quarters. There was a definite air of mystery around Jr. as the public impatiently waited for the Griscom family to return stateside. However, this early enigmatic aura would soon be replaced by a less flattering one, as the reporters dug deeper—he would come to be labeled as a lazy wastrel with questionable intentions. Jr.'s shoddy reputation took another hit when he was greeted at the docks in New York not only by the story-starved press, but by representatives from creditors, who took his luggage right out of his hands because of an outstanding bill with a merchant.

Jr.'s inauspicious return to the States, coupled with the revelations about Francis Arnold's disapproval, his thrashing by John Arnold in Florence, and his reported subservient nature to his father, shattered any previous illusions of a mysterious stranger who had Dorothy under his spell. Instead, Griscom was painted as a laughable figure who had been caught up in events beyond his control. His actions and statements to the press upon his return didn't help matters; he boasted that he was returning to the United States to find Dorothy himself. Later, he was quoted as saying he was sure her reappearance was imminent. At one point he also claimed that he intended to marry Dorothy when she resurfaced. Needless to say, none of this endeared Jr. to the Arnold family.

Despite the thrashing Jr. took in the newspapers (and from John in Italy), the Arnolds always maintained their belief that Griscom was not involved in what happened to Dorothy. In retrospect, George Griscom Jr. ended up being more of a victim of circumstances himself than a viable suspect in her disappearance. So if Jr., although juicy fodder for the tabloids, truly had nothing to do with her disappearance, what did happen to Dorothy Arnold? Griscom was the only real suspect to emerge, and he had no known motive, a watertight alibi, and was absolved of any blame by the family, private detectives, and police.

## So, What Happened to Dorothy?

Early speculation in the press included the possibility of suicide, a theory that reemerged when Griscom revealed that quite recently, Dorothy had admitted despair at her failed writing career. He thought suicide might have been a possibility. However, outside of Griscom, those who knew her best considered the very idea absurd. Even under the scrutiny of a national media storm, her close circle of family and friends consistently maintained there was no reason to think her suicidal. An examination of her circumstances tends to bear that out: She lived a privileged life in one of the world's greatest cities and seemed to understand and appreciate her good fortune. She had loving relationships with her family and a robust social life with a wide circle of friends. Even the circumstances of her final day—casually saying goodbye to her mother in the morning, planning for a party she was hosting, and conversing lightly, and for some time, with her friend outside Brentano's—hardly paint a picture of a girl about to end her life. Family spokesperson Keith summarized, "She was always happy, and her disposition was such to make foreign even a suggestion of self-destruction." Considering everything known about Dorothy's life, suicide doesn't seem a likely explanation. And if she had taken her own life, surely the body would have turned up?

While her family members had varying beliefs in the early days following her disappearance about what had happened, Francis Arnold consistently maintained that Dorothy was dead; he reasoned that if she had been able to communicate with her family, she would have. Theories of amnesia or some sort of sudden mental health crisis also didn't seem credible given the global search that had been conducted. Indeed, the whole world seemed to be looking for Dorothy Arnold. Dozens of look-alikes were reported, followed up on, and dismissed. Surely, the genuine article would have attracted some attention after appearing in newspapers coast to coast.

Though believing her dead, Dorothy's father would not commit to a theory as to how his daughter had met her fate. But when pressed, he suggested that she might have been assaulted while walking through Central Park after her shopping trip. He added, "It was my daughter's habit to walk through Central Park. She might have started up that walk between East Drive and Fifth Avenue, which is dark and unfrequented early on a winter's afternoon, or she might have taken the walk by the reservoir. There it would have been an easy matter to attack her. She might have been gagged—atrocious things do happen."

Francis argued that if Dorothy had been killed in the park, the easiest way to dispose of her body would have been to discard it in one of its many lakes and ponds; he wanted these bodies of water dragged. The police countered that it had been literally below freezing not only that day, with a temperature of 21 degrees, but also every day of the previous week. Ice-skaters were out on the solidly frozen lake the day she disappeared! After Francis met with Deputy Commissioner

Flynn, it was agreed he would use his team of private investigators, supported by the police, to comb every nook and cranny of Central Park; when the search failed to yield any clues as to Dorothy's fate, Flynn relented and ordered the park's waters dragged. Once again there was no sign of Dorothy. If she had met her end in Central Park, whoever did the dirty deed somehow had ensured the body ended up elsewhere.

While her father believed Dorothy had been killed, other members of the family were not always in steadfast agreement. Her mother and brother's trip to Florence is proof that they at least entertained the idea that Dorothy was still alive somehow. Could she have purposely vanished without a trace or a word to any family member or friend? Secret romances or elopements had often been at the root of past disappearances of society girls—the Arnolds themselves had kept the story from the press because they feared Dorothy might have run away willingly. Advocates of the theory that Dorothy purposefully ran away pointed to her forbidden relationship with Griscom and the family's attempts to initially hide, and later downplay, its existence.

Additionally, suspicion swirled around the letters from the general delivery window at the post office, used for her correspondence with publishers but also for clandestine messaging with Jr. Whom else might Dorothy have been sending messages to? A report also surfaced that a few months before Dorothy had vanished for good, she had similarly disappeared for a few days. Mr. Arnold had private detectives visit the state marriage license bureau to inquire about any marriages in the past year involving a "Miss Arnold." None were recorded in the register, and it was later discovered that Dorothy was in Washington, DC, visiting a college friend. But this incident is further proof that the family at one point suspected that Dorothy was not telling them everything about her affairs.

And yet, when one closely examines her personal life, it seems wildly out of character for her to willingly vanish without a trace, whether to hide a romantic entanglement or for some other, unknown reason. Elsie Henry, one of Dorothy's closest friends, said, "She never spoke of trouble at home, nor did she regard herself as misunderstood. If she had any romances, I knew nothing of them, and I was very intimate with her." Similar sentiments were shared by others who knew Dorothy well; in fact, she seemed to prefer spending time with her girlfriends from Bryn Mawr. "Miss Arnold was not the sort of girl to have what might be called a romance. She was a sensible girl. She had possibly a dozen men who called upon her, but she did not lose her heart to any of them," added family spokesperson John Keith.

More objectively, Dorothy's behavior in the days and weeks leading up to, and including, December 12, bely any suspicions that she had planned to run away, just as they contradict the suicide theory. Two days before she disappeared, she was out to lunch and shopping with a group of four friends. Everyone there said she was acting completely normally. Although she did apparently have a propensity to be distracted by a good book and a chocolate snack, she was out shopping for a gown for an upcoming party that she would be hosting on the day she vanished. There was no real strife between her and her family, and no clue could be found to explain why she would want to voluntarily vanish so abruptly. Finally, if she was living a new life somewhere, surely she would have been recognized by someone, as the case became a global phenomenon, and pictures of Dorothy were plastered in newspapers, magazines, pamphlets, and posters all over the world.

And so, after ruling out so many possibilities, what are we left with? Nothing that the contemporaneous investigators came up with or anything that has surfaced in the century since leaves us with anything to really go on; yet Dorothy did disappear, and so the supporting circumstances must have been extremely unusual by nature. Maybe she was abducted during a walk in Central Park and later died of her wounds, giving her assailant time to dispose of the body in the Hudson River. This is one possible scenario, although, as with other theories, there is practically no evidence to support it.

## Coda

Perhaps the most intriguing of all leads emerged a few years later, in April 1914: An undercover sting of the notorious "House of Mystery" in the suburbs of Pittsburgh revealed that Dr. C. C. Meredith had been illegally operating what was termed a "maternity hospital"—in all likelihood performing abortions, which were against the law nationwide in 1910. Dr. H. E. Lutz, an associate who claimed he had been duped by Meredith, assisted authorities with the raid and ensuing arrest. Lutz claimed that many women had come to have procedures at the large, isolated institution, which was situated on a high bluff overlooking a dark, murky river in Bellevue, Pennsylvania. Apparently, not every patient of the good Dr. Meredith survived, and Lutz claimed that these unfortunate women were disposed of in the basement furnace; according to Lutz, Meredith had once confided to him that Dorothy Arnold had met her fate here.

When asked for comment on these reports, Francis Arnold seemed like he had had enough. He said he had no knowledge of these claims and was absolutely certain that his daughter was dead after so many years. John Keith added that these were in fact not new claims; he had personally gone to the institute in 1910, demanding to see the patient there who was rumored to be Dorothy Arnold. He was shown the woman, who most assuredly was not Dorothy. Without any credible evidence beyond the secondhand claims of Dr. Lutz, and given the lack of conviction from both the authorities and the Arnolds, the theory that Dorothy had ended up in the dreaded House of Mystery never gained much traction.

And yet, perhaps the family shouldn't have given up on this theory so quickly. If Lutz was right, she would have died and been incinerated way before Keith had visited the site—that could only have happened after the story went public in late January. It would have been easy for Dr. Meredith, or any other staff at the facility, to show Keith a random woman to convince him Dorothy was not there. It should be remembered that Dorothy had been alone with George Griscom Jr. in the months before her disappearance, so the possibility that Dorothy was pregnant does exist; in fact, the location of the infamous institute was near Jr.'s home with his parents in Pittsburgh.

On the other hand, why would Dorothy have sought an abortion so haphazardly, at such a shoddy and far-off locale? She had the resources to discreetly take care of an unwanted pregnancy if that was her desire, and all existing evidence illustrates that her personality favored discretion and pragmatism. There is also no supporting evidence to the House of Mystery lead, one of the many, many theories and rumors that have emerged over the years, trying to wrestle with the unsolvable enigma that Dorothy Arnold has come to represent.

5

# Farmhouse Tragedy

## *North Greenbush*

Horatio Mould was likely annoyed as he made the drive from Rensselaer, New York, near Albany, to the more rural town of North Greenbush on the evening of Wednesday, December 11, 1911, to see what had happened to his milk delivery. Mould was driving to see Arthur Morner, who managed a local dairy farm owned and run by his widowed mother, Mary, along with the help of his two younger sisters, Blanche and Edith. *Usually*, Arthur was the one making this trip; he delivered Mould fresh cow milk from their rather prosperous farm on a daily basis. But Arthur had failed to show the prior evening. To be fair, Morner was usually a reliable sort, and Mould had initially assumed he had taken ill or perhaps had some other personal emergency arise, keeping him from their usual engagement. However, when Arthur again failed to show the subsequent night, Mould was forced to investigate for himself. Heaven forbid some sort of accident had occurred at the Morners' farm.

Easing slowly up the driveway around 8:00 p.m., Mould must have had an ominous feeling: Despite the sun having long since set, there were no lights on in the house, which was apart from the neighboring farms, sitting about one hundred feet back from the country road. He cautiously approached the front door but didn't notice anything out of the ordinary. Knocking repeatedly yielded only silence, and trying the handle revealed the place was locked from the inside. This was not the scene Mould was expecting to encounter, having known the Morner family for years, dating back to before Mary's husband, Conrad, had died a few years earlier. Something was amiss.

Mould hurried back across the road and jostled the Morners' neighbor Chester Ostrander from his nightly routine to see if he knew anything about what was happening at the farm. As far as Ostrander knew, everything was okay; his wife, Jessie, remembered last seeing the younger daughter, Blanche, going out to the barn on Tuesday afternoon. No, they hadn't seen or talked to any of the Morners since then, although there were lights on in the house last evening. Ostrander joined Mould in returning to the Morners', where a perfunctory search of the property revealed little except for dozens of cattle left unattended, grazing in the fields. They decided to fetch the eldest Morner sibling, Jesse, who lived on and operated his own farm a few miles from the main family property.

Jesse was also rightly alarmed, having no insight into any trouble his family was in or where they might be. He returned with what was slowly forming into a posse, as other neighbors learned of the potential trouble at the Morners' place. The group forced entry into the house, where things seemed calm and quiet: The housework appeared to have been recently attended to, and everything was in its proper place. Except for the missing inhabitants. The only sign of any disturbance was the door leading from the kitchen to the sitting room—it was hanging awkwardly on its hinges as if it had been roughly forced, with the woodwork splintered and part of the lock snapped off. In the sitting room there was a note written in Italian lying atop a piano. Members of the group recalled the Morners had taken on an Italian farmhand by the name of Ed Dennis, aka Edward Donato, the previous August. Donato, who boarded with the family, was also unaccounted for. When later translated, the note read, "Italian comes to America and makes sausage."

### Grisly Discovery

The party moved on to search the grounds of the farm, including the barns, where they found additional horses and cows in their pens. With more neighbors arriving as the night went on, the posse split off into groups of two or three, equipped with lanterns to comb over every square inch of the property. And yet, despite this intense late-night hunt for any sign of the Morners, their whereabouts remained elusive.

After checking and rechecking all obvious hiding places where any signs of foul play might be covertly stashed, it was Jesse Morner who suggested to the exhausted search party one overlooked spot: a refuse pit used for manure and other undesirable waste materials, which had been built under the floor of one of the cattle barns. As the party hurriedly pried the floorboards loose, two bare legs that had been held down by the planks jerked upward. The men apprehensively crept forward with lanterns lit, only to be rewarded by a sight that revolted all present: a mound of bloody and bruised bodies, distorted and crammed together in the pit to conceal discovery.

There were three bodies piled one on top of the other, embedded into the waste and refuse. Mary, the Morner matriarch, was on the top, face down. Edith, her eldest daughter, was directly beneath her, with the younger Morner girl, Blanche, at the bottom. The bodies of all three women were practically naked, their clothes having been ripped and torn from them. A bloody hatchet and a battered four-foot bale stick had also been discarded into the waste pit, seemingly the instruments of these gruesome murders. Not a word was spoken by the men, who all drew back and solemnly removed their hats.

Soon after the discovery of the women's bodies, the authorities were alerted and promptly arrived at the Morners' farm. Rensselaer County coroner Morris Strope arrived first, directing the withdrawal of the bodies from the barn and their unceremonious transfer to the cold ground outside, covered only by thin blankets for several hours until their removal could be arranged. Sheriff William Contrell, who would subsequently lead the investigation into the murders, received word of the tragedy shortly before midnight and was also soon at the crime scene with his deputies.

With law enforcement on hand, the search of the ninety-acre property intensified, and a few more potential clues were exposed. A man's watch—possibly belonging to Arthur or the farmhand, Donato—was found in another part of the stable from where the bodies were unearthed. Even more telling was the small splash of blood found on a pail a short distance from the barn at the base of a cow stanchion used for milking, likely indicating where one of the victims had been struck down; just a few feet from the bloodstain was a broken hair comb lodged in a feed box. Finally, about two hundred feet from where the bodies were found was another, larger, bloodstain, together with a few strands of black hair matted together by blood. The forensics capabilities of 1911 didn't allow for the kind of analysis of the crime scene that today's technologies and methodologies would have produced, but the evidence did show that the horrible violence inflicted upon the women found under the floorboards had likely occurred there in the same barn. Arthur Morner and Edward Donato were still unaccounted for, and the search went on until 3:00 a.m. before the exhausted men, many of whom knew the dead women, gave up for the night, vowing to renew their efforts in the morning.

Investigators resumed the search early the next day, more systematically now, with additional law enforcement officers present. As suspicion grew that

*WHERE THE MORNER FAMILY WAS MURDERED*

The Barn Five Miles From Albany, N. Y., in Which Were Found the Bodies of Mrs. Ann Morner, Her Two Daughters and Her Son, Who were Foully Slain.

BUFFALO ENQUIRER, DECEMBER 16, 1911

the missing Italian farmhand was the culprit, bloodhounds were brought in to lead the manhunt. These dogs proved instrumental in finally tracking down Arthur Morner at around 9:00 a.m. that Thursday; his body too had been hidden, crammed into a drainage well. Upon examination, his throat had been slashed and there were two large gashes on his head; the body had bruises and cuts all over. An autopsy later revealed that cause of death was a blow to the head that had simultaneously fractured his skull and broken his neck. The discovery of Arthur's body cemented Edward Donato as the likely culprit, and the Italian farmhand was still missing.

## Suspect

Edward Donato aka Ed Dennis aka Dennis di Donato aka Eduardo Donati—the many aliases Donato went by likely had to do with his Italian background, as immigrants at the time often felt compelled to "Americanize" their names to better fit in—had come to work for the Morners in early August 1911, also living with them in their home. On August 10, Arthur had gone to the Empire Employment agency, a staffing company in Albany that he had used before, looking for help in anticipation of the upcoming busy season. Donato had only just completed his application and was still in the office when Arthur walked in, and an arrangement between the two parties was quickly reached.

Donato was twenty-five years old and described as good-looking, with a smooth face and dark black hair. He had a slight build: five feet six and between 115 and 120 pounds. His prominent, darkly shaded eyes and complexion were distinguishing features. He was last seen wearing a striped suit and overcoat.

When family members and friends were asked about the man who had lived with the Morners the past few months, they foreshadowed what neighbors of future serial killers would seemingly always say, describing him as quiet, polite, industrious, and sober, someone who tended to his own business. Everyone who was asked said they knew of no ill will between Donato and the Morners, and that in fact they were on quite friendly terms. He was reportedly paid and treated very well.

Donato's background prior to coming to the Morners was largely a mystery, and a search of his room after the murders added little relevant information. Investigators did find an unaddressed letter in Italian, possibly written by Donato to his parents in Italy, as well as several letters he had received from family and friends back home. The man from the agency who had connected Donato and Arthur Morner thought the wanted man might have said he had come down the river from Poughkeepsie.

Donato was last seen around 3:30 p.m. on the day the murders were committed. He had gone to see Mrs. Mary McCann, a neighbor, requesting her assistance in mending his trousers, which had been ripped from the knee down; she also sewed several buttons on for him. Although the exact time of the murders was unknown, the bloodstain on the milk pail helped fix the time at around noon, when, it was known, the Morners were in the habit of milking their cows. This indicated that if Donato was the murderer, he had taken the time to get help mending his clothes; perhaps the pants had been ripped during the tussle with his victims, although Mrs. McCann did not recall noticing any bloodstains. Another neighbor reported seeing the lights on in both the kitchen and Donato's room until late into the evening that night, indicating that he didn't seem to be in a great hurry to get away from the horrific crime scene.

With Donato clearly the primary suspect, law enforcement pivoted their efforts to tracking him down. The same pair of bloodhounds that had helped uncover Arthur's corpse were given Donato's scent from his clothes and a pair of shoes, and the hunt was on: The hounds circled the barn where the bodies had been found a few times and then took off in a frenzy, with Sheriff Cottrell and his men following in automobiles, charging east for roughly six miles along the hard dirt road toward the tiny hamlet of West Sand Lake. The dogs continued their furious pace until they reached the tracks of the Troy & New England

Railroad trolley station, where the trail abruptly stopped. The trolley ran west into the rural countryside and northeast to the city of Troy; with such access to multiple escape routes and more than a day's head start, Donato was unlikely to be easily found.

## Madness

After the shock of the initial discovery of the bodies in the Morners' barn, Sheriff Cottrell was soon leading the hunt for the missing Italian farmhand. However, questions about what could have led to the horrific murders were soon at the forefront of investigators' thoughts. Assuming Donato was the killer, newspapers carried headlines ascribing insanity as his motivation for committing such atrocities; the note written in Italian about "American sausage" would certainly seem to indicate that Donato's mental state was a factor.

There was also speculation about robbery being a motive; accordingly, it was thought that a burglar—Donato or someone else—might have been caught in the act, leading to a struggle with Arthur Morner, with the women killed subsequently to cover the burglar's escape. The Morners were quite prosperous for farmers—as heir to the Morner estate, Jesse inherited $12,225 (approximately $400,000 in 2025 dollars). Donato had been living on the farm long enough to have some knowledge of their finances and where the Morners might have kept their money. The robbery theory lost favor when it was reported that $600 had been found on the premises after the house was searched.

Perhaps the biggest clue to the killer's motive came from the autopsies. Arthur had been battered to death with the bale stick; his skull was fractured and his neck snapped, with the two large gashes on his head highlighting where the fatal blows were struck. His throat had also been slashed. The bodies of all three women had many cuts and bruises, indicating each had been involved in a struggle before being killed. Mary had received a blow from the hatchet on the right side of her head, cutting a great gash deep through her skull, which was fractured at multiple points. The elder sister, Edith, had a large hole in her left temple, and her head had been nearly severed from her body. One of her arms was broken, and both arms were positioned in front of her, as if in fear or for protection. Blanche's body was the least bruised and lacerated, but perhaps most significantly, the autopsy revealed she had been raped before being murdered. This revelation superseded the other nascent theories, and the prevailing wisdom was now that the other murders were part of an attempt to cover up Blanche's initial rape and murder.

## Manhunt

As Sheriff Cottrell and his deputies questioned those at the trolley station in Sand Lake, they found a conductor who remembered seeing a man matching Donato's description. The man had boarded a car with five cents asking to go to Troy; as the fare to Troy was ten cents, the conductor dropped him off at Snyder's Corners, a stop along the way. Cottrell and his men charged ahead, with the hounds picking up the scent again at the Snyder's Corners stop. They continued to trail the fugitive to a barn on the outskirts of Troy, where it was thought he had spent the night. The hunt continued onward, but the scent became faint nearer the city and finally was lost.

In 1911, Troy was a thriving metropolis with roads, trolleys, train tracks, and even waterways leading north to Canada and south to New York City and then to destinations in every direction beyond. Indeed, an early rumor had a man answering Donato's description applying at the People's Line docks in Albany on the day after the murders for permission to work his way to New York City on the steamer *C. W. Morse*; as a man was needed, he was taken aboard, but when the steamer was met by police as it docked, it turned out to be a false alarm, the first of many in the case.

Considering the wanted man's options after arriving in Troy following his flight from the Morners' farm, authorities thought he might still be nearby and put out alerts to neighboring cities. In Buffalo, an Italian man in a black suit who appeared to be in his mid-thirties was arrested based on his erratic behavior at the city's Central Station. He gave his name as Tony Mori and said he was from Syracuse; police detained Mori until officers arrived from Albany to speak with, and, subsequently, release him, as there was no evidence to hold him.

In Port Chester, New York, close to the Connecticut border, Bernardino Nabilo was arrested not only for being Italian, but also for hailing from Pittsfield, which rumors said Donato had been making for. However, the most damning piece of evidence—a bloodstained handkerchief found in Nabilo's pocket—turned out to be the result of an innocuous nosebleed. When a description of Donato was later clarified by authorities in Troy, it turned out Nabilo looked nothing like the man.

An Italian man from Mechanicsville who gave his name initially as Charles Alli and later as Antonio Cerato was arrested after he was found sleeping at the Williamstown railroad station. The night operator had noticed him acting "strangely," and when questioned the man gave conflicting reports about his recent whereabouts. Despite this "strong" evidence against Alli, he was also ultimately cleared and released.

As this parade of early suspects were detained only to be absolved one by one because of a lack of evidence or by witnesses who had personally known Donato, competing theories emerged regarding what had happened on the Morners' farm: Could the missing Italian farmhand actually have been another victim?

Seeking fresh evidence, the police revisited the crime scene, ripping up the floorboards in all of the barns in their quest to find additional human remains. There was no trace of Donato, but District Attorney Abbott Jones helped fuel the theory that someone other than Donato had committed the murders by declaring that the handwriting of the chilling note about making American sausage found in the Morners' home, presumably left by the murderer, was different from samples of Donato's. However, Sherriff Cottrell disagreed with the DA over the handwriting; he also believed that Donato may have stolen money from the house, either as partial motive behind the killings or after the fact, as he was preparing to flee. Although $600 had been found in the house, it was later clarified that the money had been hidden in Mary Morner's bed, a secret location that any burglar would have been unlikely to know about.

Jesse Morner, whose mother, two sisters and brother were murdered at their farmhouse near Albany, N. Y. Jesse is leading the search for the murderer.

BUFFALO ENQUIRER

With Donato's whereabouts—either dead or alive—unknown, some questioned whether Jesse Morner, the surviving member of the family, was involved in the murders. On the surface, Jesse, the sole heir to the Morner estate, appeared to be a credible suspect who at least had to be considered. On the afternoon of Monday, December 18, the day after the Morners' funeral reception was held at their farm, Sherriff Cottrell and Assistant District Attorney Timothy Quillinan summoned Jesse for questioning back at his family's home. On his way in to speak with the investigators, he was ambushed by reporters wanting to know his thoughts on being considered a suspect. Jesse had naturally taken the murders hard, and since the discovery of the bodies had seemed to be almost lost in a haze. He was unnerved as he responded to the press; the strain of the slayings, in addition to his responsibility for the upkeep of his mother's farm while maintaining his own, was clearly showing.

Jesse, the oldest Morner son, took after his late father, Conrad; both men were industrious, detail oriented, and naturally reserved. Jesse took pride in being known as a hard worker, rarely taking time off for pleasure. His family and friends quickly came to his defense when the allegations emerged, decrying any such claims as ridiculous. While Jesse was never known for his social graces—one neighbor who knew him for years said the most he heard him ever talk was to bid him the time of day and then go about his business—he stayed close to his family and always found time to visit his mother, who admired Jesse's industrious nature and constantly worried that he was working too hard.

Despite his outrage at the aspersions cast upon him, Jesse retained his composure while facing a barrage of questions from Sheriff Cottrell and his team: Was he friendly with Donato? More so than usual for a farmhand? How often did he visit his parents' home? Did he suspect Donato of foul play? What made him suggest looking under the floorboards in the barn, where the dead bodies were eventually found?

The interrogation was extensive, digging back into details from when his father was still alive. There were also rumors that his mother owned his property and that he had been left out of his deceased family's wills. He denied these rumors and answered all questions put to him freely and frankly, showing no emotion, even when probed about the intimate details of the relationships within the Morner family. He went so far as to invite investigators to search his home for anything amiss. Cottrell and the district attorney's office came away impressed with Jesse's candor—it seemed he was as innocent of the crime as was his deceased brother, Arthur. And so, with other leads having dried up, the focus returned to tracking down Edward Donato.

## FUGITIVE

As the hunt for Donato continued, his background as an immigrant would continue to play a significant role in events, as Italian communities were heavily targeted in trying to track the wanted man down. At the time of the Morners' murders, America was in the midst of a surge of Italian immigration, fueled by economic difficulties in Europe and the promise of better prospects overseas. As is often the case, this wave of immigration had the unfortunate side effect of arousing anti-Italian feelings in certain segments of the population.

The informal segregation that ethnic groups were delineated into during the early twentieth century allowed for a targeted investigation as to where Donato might be: Newspapers of the time spoke of "Italian colonies" being searched, as if these ethnic neighborhoods were the secret beachheads of rival foreign empires. The investigation would go on to yield many additional suspects, usually based on little more than an Italian man arousing suspicion with "unusual behavior" or even by merely showing up in a place where someone didn't recognize him—this intrusion into the Italian community was only worsened when the initial description of Donato sent out via the press was completely incorrect.

One lead that showed promise came from Hudson, New York, about forty-five miles south of Troy. A Hudson city patrolman claimed to have spoken to Donato at around 5:00 a.m. on the day after the murders were supposed to have been committed. The officer was said to have known Donato previously, and the description he provided of the man he spoke to matched Donato's before it had even been made public. The patrolman said Donato had seemed anxious, with bloodshot eyes, as if he hadn't been sleeping well, and asked the officer about the train to Pittsfield, Massachusetts. The train wasn't due for a few hours, so he departed, saying he was going to wait at a friend's house. When officers later arrived at his friend's house, the suspect had already departed, leaving his overcoat behind in his hurried exit.

With the trail gone cold again, police targeted the suspect's supposed destination, Pittsfield, northeast from Hudson and Springfield, where a man matching Donato's description had been seen the night after the murders. Cottrell and his team spent time in both cities, but every potential suspect was eventually cleared.

In the small town of Coxsackie, about thirty miles south of Troy, another Italian immigrant who matched Donato's description was arrested two days after the murders. The proprietor of the Cobblestone Inn in Coxsackie had spoken to the man, who said he had just arrived in town around noon that day and was looking for work as a railway hand. With his hackles aroused by the man's vague background—the Italian refused to give his name initially—not to mention the promise of the recently posted $1,000 reward, the inn's owner alerted Coxsackie authorities, who upon questioning the suspect found letters in his pocket signed "Di Donato," although these had been sent *to him* from the village of Lowville, New York.

The Coxsackie police held the man overnight until he could be transported to the Rensselaer County Jail in Troy by Sheriff Cottrell. En route to Troy, the man encountered a rough scene at Union Station in Albany around 4:00 a.m. Cottrell and his deputies met the car that was escorting the suspect, which was quickly surrounded by hundreds of people who had been following the case in the newspapers. While many were there because they were angry about the murders, many others were there to show support for the Italian, who had been arrested based on little evidence.

As the crowd grew ever more aggravated, the suspect was aggressively confronted by John J. Bonacker, a family friend of the Morners, who had accompanied Cottrell: "I've seen you before," accused Bonacker. The Italian was nonplussed, "You never saw me before." "I haven't, eh?" Bonacker retorted, as the unruly crowd surged forward. Aware of the escalating situation, the officers rushed the man to Cottrell's waiting car, which quickly sped off as the crowd hurled angry threats at the escaping suspect.

In Troy, Assistant DA Quillinan grilled the man for over an hour and a half with the aid of a translator. He first gave his name as Samuel Raymond, but later added the alias Sammio Saveni, another example of immigrants of the era using multiple pseudonyms. The interrogation yielded little else in terms of useful information, as Raymond denied all knowledge of or involvement in the murders.

Later that morning, Miss Vera Vandenberg, who was friendly with the Morner daughters and had known Donato from visits to their farm, arrived at the jail escorted by a deputy sheriff to identify the suspect. She gave Raymond one glance and immediately declared, "That's not him." With nothing concrete to hold the man, Raymond was given breakfast and escorted back to Albany; there, officials once again arrested him, holding him for a final round of questioning before finally returning him to Coxsackie. That same day, John Bonacker, still convinced the man was Edward Donato, arrived at the jail in Troy, bringing Horatio Mould, the milk dealer who had initiated the discovery of the Morners' bodies when he came looking for a delinquent Arthur; Bonacker was hoping Mould would confirm his suspicions about the identity of the man being held. Instead, police informed him that Samuel Raymond was no longer a party of interest in the case and had been set free.

## Desperation

In March 1912, months after the murders, yet another Italian was detained, in Long Island City; this time the accusations were more credible than those lodged against the immigrants who had been arrested for merely being an Italian someone didn't recognize. Bartholomew Salerno had drifted from town to town seeking employment until finally settling in Long Island City in December, finding work as a sand-truck driver for a contractor named Louis Ferger. Ferger, who had no complaints about Salerno's work, did notice that he didn't mingle much with the other Italians he employed. At one point he heard rumors from his men that Salerno and another Italian driver had had a conversation about murdering Ferger and running off with the large cash roll that he kept in the office. The other man responded to Salerno's proposal, asking, "What can we do with the body?" The suspect allegedly said, "Put him under the boards in the stable. No one will know."

Ferger's suspicions were further aroused when he read about the Morners' murders and concluded that Salerno seemed to match the description of Edward Donato. He consulted with a lawyer, who contacted the authorities in Troy; they provided a more detailed description of Donato: It was a close match except Salerno had a mustache whereas Donato was clean shaven. However, it was later clarified that he had started growing the mustache only after coming to work for Ferger in December.

Most damning of all was a small notebook found in Salerno's pocket when he was arrested. The name Bartholomew Salerno was written several times in the front of the notebook, as if someone had been practicing their handwriting; more ominously, in the very back of the book was written the name Dennis di Donato, one of Donato's aliases, and the name the Morners knew him by.

Under intense questioning by newly elected District Attorney Clarence Akin, Salerno denied any knowledge of the crimes. He claimed to have found the notebook with Donato's name already written in the back when he was out for a walk collecting driftwood. Salerno went on to explain that he was learning to write English, and the jottings of his name in the front of the book were actually those of a neighbor's son who was tutoring him. As had now become routine when a suspect was arrested, several family members and friends who had known Edward Donato personally, including Jesse Morner, came to see the suspect; while they admitted the resemblance was close, none were willing to identify him as the man they were seeking.

## Justice

More arrests followed in the months ahead, but they became less frequent as time passed, until ultimately it was apparent that the Morners' killer would evade justice. If Edward Donato was guilty of the crimes, what had happened to him after he had fled from the scene? Even if Bartholomew Salerno had no connection to the case, the notebook he found could have been lost there by Donato. If so, it would confirm early fears that Donato had been able to lose himself in New York City after fleeing from Troy.

His ultimate fate may have been revealed in the letter found in his room at the Morners' farm that he had been writing to his parents back in Italy. Donato wrote of his dissatisfaction with living in the United States—many Italian immigrants came to the States solely to earn money to send back to their family, before eventually returning home themselves. Maybe the killer was able to sneak back to Europe on one of the many cruisers regularly crisscrossing the Atlantic during this era. Perhaps after fleeing the farm, Donato returned to Italy and joined the army, as his letter home had indicated was his desire. The Italians were in the midst of a series of colonial misadventures in North Africa, clashing over territory with the remnants of the Ottoman Empire. If so, and if there was any balance of justice for the grotesque slaying of the Morner family, perhaps his life ended on some forgotten battlefield in an equally pointless manner.

# 6

# A Bridge Too Far

## *New York City*

Death was not proud on June 11, 1920, when it came to forty-four-year-old Joseph Bowne Elwell, a vain, libidinous reprobate—and nationally known bridge player—who was shot once in the forehead as he sat in a plushly upholstered chair in the drawing room of his four-story granite-front home on the Upper West Side of Manhattan. Elwell, by all accounts a notorious amorist, was reliably reported to have bedded some fifty women, many of them married, and his chauffeur would testify that he regularly ordered him to stop the car so that he could proposition random women walking along the street; if they turned him down, he simply claimed he had mistaken them for someone else. At the time of his death, he was barefoot and garbed only in red silk pajamas, his shiny bald head uncovered by the toupee he would absolutely never allow himself to be seen in public without, his false teeth soaking in a whiskey flask in an upstairs bathroom.

The *New York Times* called Elwell's murder "among the most remarkable in the annals of crime in this country," and not just because of a monumentally futile investigation led by a district attorney with a checkered history of his own. Elwell counted Vanderbilts among his friends and was by marriage related to a Roosevelt, and the narrative that unfolded over the course of the ten-month investigation that followed was, to quote Sam Spade, the stuff that dreams are made of—as long as you write headlines for a tabloid newspaper. Polish countess accused of espionage? Check. Mysterious "Woman in Black"? Check. Mysterious "Woman in Gray"? Check. Mysterious "Kimono Girl"? Check. Pink silk negligee, monogram excised, smuggled out of Elwell's house to protect the identity of its owner? Check. Feuding girlfriends, feuding investigators, bootleggers, enraged men alleged to have run the victim out of one town or another upon discovering he was bedding the woman in their lives? Check, check, check, and check again.

Joseph Bowne Elwell . . . chances are you never heard of him. But in his time he enjoyed quite a reputation: bon vivant, friend to the rich and famous, renowned expert at whist and auction bridge (direct forerunners of the modern game of bridge), author (maybe), racehorse owner, and, finally, victim in one of the most sensational—and baffling—murders in the annals of New York crime. Born in Cranford, New Jersey, in 1873, Elwell was the son of Jane "Jennie" Annetta Ames and Joseph Sanford Elwell, a traveling salesman. The family moved to Brooklyn in 1879, and thanks to a wealthy relative, he attended Phillips Andover Academy near Boston from the ages of thirteen to sixteen, leaving just before his senior year for reasons that remain unclear (his future wife would claim he was expelled). He worked first as a salesman at a hardware store, then as an insurance clerk and agent. He learned to play whist at a young men's social club in church and was so masterful at it that before long he was known as the "Wizard of Whist."

In 1899, Elwell met twenty-three-year-old Helen Derby, who hailed from a prominent family, and on May 26, 1900, the two wed; soon, Helen, who would become something of a whist/bridge expert herself, mentioned to her husband that summertime in Newport, Rhode Island, was a swell place to vacation, especially if you were looking to make a bundle off wealthy folks with prodigious amounts of leisure time and a keen interest in mastering whist and bridge, which had become quite trendy among the beau monde. So off they went to Newport, where Helen leveraged her family name to procure Joseph a roster of students including members of the Vanderbilt family. Once back in New York, Elwell was playing and winning big—as much as $30,000 a night—at the city's most prestigious social clubs. Soon he was investing heavily in the stock market and real estate and bought a half share in a stable of racehorses. By the time of his death, he owned a yacht, five automobiles, a $200,000 trust fund, and over a hundred parcels of land.

The business-savvy Helen reached out to Charles Scribner's Sons to suggest a book written by her husband, and in 1902 *Elwell on Bridge* was published (rumors were that Helen ghostwrote a chunk of it); more books followed, and Elwell landed a gig penning a bridge column for the *Evening Telegram*. In 1904, Helen gave birth to a son, Richard, their only child. But trouble was brewing in the marriage. During the pregnancy, Elwell traveled to Lexington, Kentucky; as he was entering a cab outside his hotel, a young woman took a shot at him (but missed) before escaping into the gathering crowd. By 1911, he and Helen were living apart, and by 1914 he had set in motion plans for a legal separation. A year later he drew up a will leaving his entire estate to his parents, completely shutting out his wife and son.

In 1916, their separation became official. Helen angled for $5,000 a year in alimony but settled for $2,400, plus $600 a year for Richard's education at Buckley, a prestigious private school, and an additional $200 for summer camp.

And then, in 1920, Joseph Elwell's luck ran out.

## THURSDAY, JUNE 10, 1920

Elwell dines at the rooftop restaurant of the Ritz-Carlton hotel, accompanied by good buddy Walter Lewisohn, a ridiculously wealthy banker; Lewisohn's wife, Selma; Selma's sister, Viola Kraus; and Octavio Figureoa, an Argentine newspaper publisher in town for business. Earlier that day, Kraus's divorce from Victor von Schlegell, vice president of the United and Globe Rubber Company, became official, ending their four-year marriage. Elwell sits beside Kraus, who for some unknown reason becomes cross with him, extracting a pencil from her purse and scribbling something (never revealed) on the cuff of his shirt.

Who else should then show up at the rooftop restaurant but Victor von Schlegell, a comely young blonde attached to his arm. Von Schlegell will swear throughout the investigation that his appearance was merely happenstance rather than an attempt to harass his ex-wife by showing off his date, who, we should probably add here, is the mysterious "Woman in Black," meaning a black chiffon dress and black hat, whose name von Schlegell will initially claim he can't remember even though he dines and dances with her that night and breakfasts with her the following morning.

Twice during the night von Schlegell and Elwell cross paths, once in the checkout room and once on the dance floor. "Hello, Joe," von Schlegell says once the music stops. According to von Schlegell, Elwell acknowledges the greeting, but Walter Lewisohn says Elwell simply ignores him. Elwell skedaddles first, around 11:00 p.m., to purchase tickets to *Ziegfeld's Midnight Frolic* at the New Amsterdam Theatre, where the others meet up with him. After the show, they make plans to gather the following day for a trip to Long Island. It's now sometime between 1:30 and 2:00 a.m. The Lewisohns, Kraus, and Figureoa hop in a car and head home. Elwell, for reasons never publicly revealed, doesn't join them. He is last seen heading west on Forty-second Street on foot.

PHOTO COURTESY OF THE *MOUNT VERNON ARGUS*

Exactly what happens in the hours that follow is a mystery to this day, over a hundred years later.

## Friday, June 11, 1920

Housekeeper Marie Larsen reaches the Elwell residence at 244 West Seventieth Street sometime between 8:20 and 8:35 a.m. Carpenters already are at work next door, banging away and making a racket. She unlocks the double front door, steps inside the vestibule, smells cigarette smoke. She bends down to pick up the pint of milk and half pint of cream milkman Just Otten had delivered about two hours earlier. She passes the drawing room on her way to the dining room, removes her wrap, then heads back to the drawing room to begin setting the house in order. She's surprised to see Elwell sitting in the upholstered chair pressed against the wall, dressed in pajamas, no toupee. His chin rests against his chest, and the back of his head leans against the top of the chair. His feet are bare. She's maybe not the most perceptive person in the world, because she apologizes for intruding. No response. Sleeping, perhaps? She moves closer, peers into his eyes. Definitely not sleeping. His forehead is bleeding, and about three inches above his head, a bullet protrudes from the plaster wall.

The good news (perhaps) is that Elwell is still breathing.

Marie Larsen springs into action. Out on the street, she finds Otten, the milkman, who, according to which version of history you choose to believe, either does nothing (Larsen's) or alerts the superintendent of a neighboring apartment building (his). Marie waylays Patrolman Harry Singer, telling him her employer has been shot. Singer takes one look at Elwell and immediately thinks suicide. But where's the gun? Singer calls it into the station. Stay put, Captain Thomas Walsh tells him; help is on the way. Singer returns to the drawing room, surveys the situation: an open letter, smeared with blood (a report from Lloyd Gentry, Elwell's head trainer in Kentucky), on the floor beside the chair; a .45-caliber

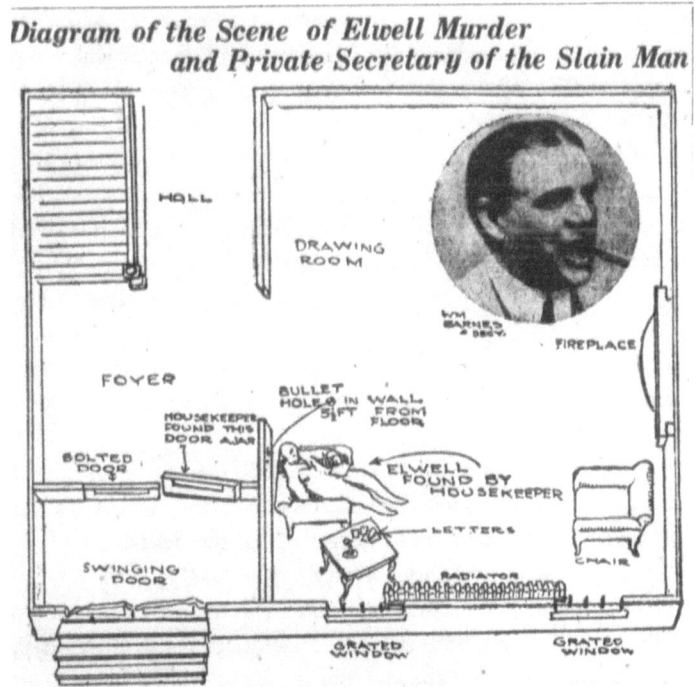

PHOTO COURTESY OF THE *EVENING WORLD*

cartridge, also on the floor; the bullet embedded in the plaster. Forget the suicide theory. Elwell is rushed to the hospital, admitted at 9:19 a.m., pronounced dead circa 10:00 a.m. He dies without making a statement or leaving any clue as to the identity of his killer.

Police digging through the house find Elwell's clothes from the night before, $400 in cash, and a scattering of jewelry, ruling out robbery as a motive. A glance at the bed suggests Elwell had probably laid down on it but not pulled back the covers. Back in the drawing room, Marie Larsen points out that an easy chair, usually pressed against a corner, has been moved; maybe the killer hid behind it waiting for Elwell to enter? A half-smoked cigarette, Elwell's custom brand, is found at his side, the wrong end having been lit (perhaps Elwell was too vexed to notice). Another half-smoked cigarette—different brand—is on the mantelpiece, still moist. Fingerprint experts turn up nothing of note. A heavy-caliber gun points to either a male shooter or, less likely, a female who knows her way around pistols. The perfectly fired shot and flawless execution suggest a cool killer experienced in the use of firearms, maybe a military vet.

Dr. Charles N. Norris, chief medical examiner, estimates Elwell was shot between 8:20 and 8:25 a.m. The bullet entered Elwell's forehead, passed out the back of his head, and lodged in the wall behind the chair where Elwell was found. Norris says Elwell was shot while sitting in the chair and lost consciousness immediately. Judging by the powder grains embedded in Elwell's forehead over an area three inches wide, the muzzle was over a foot from his forehead. An examination of the soles of Elwell's feet shows hardly a trace of dust on the skin, indicating he had taken just a few steps before he was murdered (the stairs and bedrooms are carpeted; the hall and reception room are not). Norris believes "Elwell was not taken by surprise, at least that the presence of the man or woman in the house was not a surprise to him. He might have been shot without knowing that he was about to be shot. On the other hand, he might have been sitting there, trying to induce the murderer not to shoot. There are no indications one way or another on that point."

Both Just Otten, the milkman, and Charles Torrey, the postman, say the double front doors were unlocked when they made their deliveries, yet Larsen had to unlock them to get in. So someone locked the doors between 7:25 a.m. and 8:30-ish—perhaps Elwell, after retrieving the mail?

At 11:15 a.m., the phone rings. The caller, a woman, asks to speak to Elwell; Larsen tells her he has met with a "terrible accident." Just after noon, the caller, a well-dressed young woman, shows up at the Elwell house in a cab and meets with Walsh for two hours. Police refer to her as Miss Ellis, but it's a fake name, to guard her privacy. The press eventually outs her as Florence Ellenson of Lake George, New York, who met Elwell in Palm Beach, Florida, the previous winter. According to Ellenson, Elwell posed as a divorced man, while in fact he was only separated. He had invited her to reconnect with him in Saratoga Springs, New York, once the racing season began. Elwell was supposed to call her before 8:15 a.m. on June 11 to firm up a place and time, and when he didn't, she phoned him instead.

No connection to the murder, says Detective Thomas Donohue.

Another young woman shows up at the Elwell house. She enters through the open doors, heads upstairs, runs into Larsen on her way down. This isn't the first time they've met. The woman is agitated. "What accident?" she asks Larsen. She continues up the stairs but, seeing police sniffing around, heads back down and exits the house. This is the woman authorities will soon refer to as Miss Wilson, but that too is an alias. At 1:00 p.m., Walter Lewisohn calls the house, wondering if Elwell is ready for their trip to Long Island. That ain't happening. When told the news, he, his wife, and Viola Kraus rush over. Kraus shares that she called Elwell at 2:30 a.m. that day—purpose never revealed—and he seemed "perfectly normal, not nervous in the least."

Edwin Rhodes, Elwell's chauffeur, tells authorities his boss handed out keys to the house to female acquaintances like candy on Halloween. Arthur Bishop, his former chauffeur, estimates that between seven and a dozen women had keys to Elwell's house. Most of them, he believed, were married, young, and nubile.

## SATURDAY, JUNE 12, 1920

Detectives are dispatched to the Belmont Park racetrack to interview anyone acquainted with Elwell, especially a "beautiful woman" whose daughter had been on "intimate terms" with Elwell, as the *New York Times* phrases it. The mom had just found out about the relationship; might she have been angry enough to put a bullet in Elwell's forehead, or hire someone else to do it?

William Barnes, Elwell's secretary, insists his boss was killed by "somebody with whom he was intimately acquainted. The slayer either entered the house with a key which had been previously provided by Mr. Elwell or was admitted by Mr. Elwell a few minutes before the shooting." Barnes says he has witnessed Elwell "lose as much as $50,000 without the slightest emotion. He was so calm in his demeanor that even if he knew the murderer was pointing a pistol at him, he would continue reading, just as there is evidence he was doing when he was shot. He was naturally a jovial man, and even though his murder [was threatening him], he readily would view the situation as a joke." Barnes is certain

Elwell wasn't expecting a visitor, because "he would always take off his toupee and remove his false teeth just before going to bed. From my knowledge of him, it would be absolutely impossible for him to do that if there was anyone in the house with him. It shows positively to me that he was ready for bed when he went to the door in answer to the bell and that he was not expecting a visitor." Police, too, figure Elwell recognized the killer and let him in without suspecting his life was in danger. They think Elwell voluntarily sat down and started to read his mail before the shot was fired. But Elwell's head was slightly thrown back, so they believe he had enough warning to raise his eyes from the letter to the murderer.

## MONDAY, JUNE 14, 1920

What kind of murder mystery would it be without a Polish countess suspected of spying? Investigators summon Countess Sonia de Szinawska, who had been detained for two months by the feds during World War I on suspicion of being an enemy agent. Guess who allegedly turned her in? Joseph Bowne Elwell. The countess and her sister, Amelia Hardy, were good friends with Elwell at the time. The two sisters can't imagine why Elwell would have reported the countess, even if he was a member of the American Protective League. In fact, they say, Elwell said he reached out to officials in Washington to help secure her release. "Joe Elwell was no worse than most men," the countess says. "The only difference is that his affairs are being exposed."

Victor von Schlegell gets the third degree. His story—as related by the press—is that he and the "Woman in Black" left the Ritz-Carlton at about 9:45 p.m. He took her back to her apartment, then went home himself. The following morning the two breakfasted together at von Schlegell's apartment, after which he left for Atlantic City on a prearranged business trip; hence, authorities had been unable to find him. Contradicting von Schlegell's earlier account, he and his date, whose name he reluctantly shares with authorities but pleads with them to keep secret, strolled from the Ritz-Carlton back to his place, followed by a night together in the sack. According to von Schlegell, the two plan to marry. After breakfast, he called Willet Garage and asked that his car be ready—immediately—for his trip to Atlantic City.

## TUESDAY, JUNE 15, 1920

The *New York Times* is calling this case "more baffling and insoluble than any crime of consequence in the history of NY." So baffling and insoluble, in fact, that District Attorney Edward Swann steps in to take the reins. This is maybe good news, maybe not. Swann has a checkered career, having served as a US representative and General Sessions judge, but he's a Tammany Hall politician who in 1917 was charged with filing false recommendations for the discharge of bail for defendants indicted for crimes stemming from a labor dispute. He was also charged with attempting to coerce and intimidate a witness. In 1919, the grand jury requested that Swann, now district attorney, be replaced because he was impeding the investigation into a labor strike. On October 13, 1920, the judiciary committee of the New York Bar Association will denounce Swann's candidacy for the New York State Supreme Court: "Mr. Swann's record in Congress was not noteworthy, and his services as a Judge of the Court of General Sessions was not adequate."

A teary-eyed Marie Larsen, who has been insisting all along that she left everything in the Elwell house untouched, is now saying . . . just kidding! While police congregated in the drawing room on the morning of the murder, she slipped upstairs to hide a pink silk negligee (monogram excised), slippers, and a boudoir cap. The press is now referring to the negligee as a kimono, which it is not. When police eventually discover her subterfuge, she swears she acted on her own, because, she says, "I thought it would not be nice for them to be found there." While she initially claims she doesn't know the owner's name, she's lying; it's the same woman Larsen had run into on the stairway the morning of the murder. Soon afterward, John Dooling, the assistant district attorney, announces that the woman has been identified, but he will refer to her only as Miss Wilson. Reporters soon figure out Miss Wilson is really Viola Kraus, after a detective lets slip that she was the same woman who had called Elwell at 2:30 a.m. the day of the murder. Larsen hides the garments in a gray cardboard box squirreled away in a closet in Elwell's bedroom. Authorities don't seem especially perturbed. "It was just a matter of one woman protecting another," says Swann. Reporters track down Larsen's husband at his butcher shop, where he's asking customers if they think his wife's newfound celebrity will boost sales of meat. Kraus, meanwhile, is vying with Marie Larsen for the title of least reliable narrator, claiming she hadn't been to Elwell's house more than a couple of times. "I always thought Mr. Elwell a nice fellow, but he did not have the least attraction for me sentimentally."

Police have been driving themselves loony trying to figure out Elwell's timeline after leaving the New Amsterdam at approximately 1:45 a.m. on June 11. Assuming Kraus is telling the truth, he was home by 2:30 a.m., when she spoke to him by phone. But John Isdale, two doors from Elwell, steps forward with another story, saying he couldn't catch a wink that night because of the oppressive heat. At 3:45 a.m. he heard the rumblings of a sports car, got up, peered out the window, and saw Elwell exit the car and wave to the driver, who took off as Elwell entered his house.

A posse of detectives heads for Lexington, Kentucky, following reports that Elwell had been threatened by a relative of Anne Russell Griffy, who had met Elwell during the two weeks he spent at the Latonia racetrack before returning to New York. According to this story, Elwell bolted Lexington under threat of being shot because of his affair with the Kentucky woman. Griffy chastises reporters in tears, insisting that neither her father nor brother know anything of Elwell or her acquaintance with him. Wondering how Elwell found enough hours in the day for all these dalliances? That's nothing. William Barnes tells Swann his boss had been intimate with at least fifty women—and those are just the ones he knows about.

So how would Edward Swann rate his first day on the job? "There is no doubt that it is a murder, not a suicide," he says. "But the motive is absolutely unknown to us. Clues to the identity of the murderer are absolutely lacking. Nothing has been discovered to cause us even to suspect anybody."

"Boys," Swann adds, "it's the mystery case of the century."

### WEDNESDAY, JUNE 16, 1920

Cabdriver Philip Bender comes forward to say he picked up the Lewisohn party outside the New Amsterdam on June 10 and drove them home. Nothing very dramatic there, but Bender insists he had three passengers: two men and a woman. "I'll bet my wagon that there were only three in the car," he says. Did Viola Kraus stay behind with Elwell?

Helen Derby Elwell, the victim's estranged widow, sits for her first in-depth interview, with the *New York* Times. She grumbles about life without servants and carps at her raffish in-laws, who have no appreciation for fine art.

Elwell and his wife had barely seen or talked to each other since 1912, four years before their official separation. They had lived in the same house, but in different rooms. They rarely ate together. He might come home at 2:00 a.m. or he might come home at 7:00 a.m. or he might not call home at all, but the common denominator is he never felt obliged to inform his wife which one it would be. She's certain Elwell was bedding other women.

Asked how she managed to eke by on a "measly" $200 a month, Helen replies, "I didn't. Accustomed to all the luxuries as I was, it was no easy matter for me to get along alone.... After having five or six servants in our Park Ave home, I'm forced to get along here without any at all." Since the separation, she says, she hadn't seen her husband at all and received just two letters from him, one in response to her request to move Richard to Andover (go for it, he said) and one, on May 27, asking if she was amenable to a divorce. You betcha, she wrote back. Anything to end their "marital unhappiness." She also took the occasion to mention that the lease on her apartment was expiring in October, and what exactly did he plan to do about it?

According to Helen Elwell, this wasn't the first time the subject of divorce came up. "Just after we became separated, I asked Mr. Elwell if he didn't think it best we got a divorce decree immediately," she said. "After only a second's hesitation he replied that he thought that would be an unwise step because, he said, I was a great help to him. I realize very well what he meant. If I were divorced from him, he could perhaps have got into trouble with his women friends and could have been sued for breach of promise. I do not know what the chances were, but it could not happen while I was still his wife, and he knew it."

Now Elwell had apparently changed his mind; they'd planned a trip to Reno, but Elwell's murder deep-sixed all that.

## THURSDAY, JUNE 17, 1920

Newspapers are reporting the DA's office believes it knows both who killed Elwell and why, but Swann labels the reports "entirely without foundation." Von Schlegell admits that he keeps a pistol in his apartment, he's never fired it, he doesn't know what caliber it is (.38, so not the .45 that killed Elwell), and he doesn't know if he has a permit for it, which means he doesn't. The press clearly dislikes the guy, because it keeps harassing Swann to arrest him for it.

PHOTO COURTESY OF
*THE PUNXSUTAWNEY SPIRIT*

William A. Pendleton, Elwell's erstwhile partner in the racehorse business, is miffed at Marie Larsen, scoffing at her contention that Elwell once, the previous winter, left the key to the front door under the mat for him so that he could enter the house on business in Elwell's absence. "The statement credited to Mrs. Larsen is perfectly absurd. She does not know what she is talking about. I had not seen Elwell for eight months or more, when I had dinner with him one evening. I never was very intimate with him, for I am a family man and could not afford to run about with him." So Elwell wasn't a family man?

ADAs John Dooling and John Joyce may share a first name, but they can't stand each other. "I have been on this case from the beginning and in charge of this investigation," Joyce says. "If Dooling steps into this case, I will step out." Responds Dooling, rather cooly: "Judge Swann has charge of this case, and we are simply aiding him."

## Friday, June 18, 1920

Swann may be in charge, but he has nothing to show for it. "I will make a very candid statement," he tells the press. "We are as far from the solution as we were on Friday morning when the crime was committed."

A Woman in Black . . . a Kimono Girl . . . now meet our newest *femme mystérieuse*: A Woman in Gray. Marie Larsen testifies that this woman was the last person to call on Elwell at home before his death, on Tuesday, June 8. She's described as a "little, short, fat, dark-haired pretty girl of about twenty-four who wore a gray dress that was trimmed with fur at the bottom" (this woman is never publicly identified). After spending two and a half hours with Elwell, she left in a cab. There's some confusion over whether Larsen got her dates wrong or whether cabdriver Joseph Wagstaff referred to a different woman that he drove from Elwell's house to a shop on Madison Avenue the day before. So many women! Dooling reveals the "Woman in Gray" has been identified but refuses to reveal her name.

"Has she any connection with the murder?" Dooling is asked.

"I would not say anything about her except that she has been identified."

Now, about those keys to the house that Elwell so generously passed out to female acquaintances: forget about it . . . maybe. It turns out the lock of the inner door was changed the previous December following an attempted burglary, and according to Larsen—possibly the least reliable witness on the planet—she and Elwell had the only two keys that fit the new lock. William Barnes still isn't convinced, and who knows if Elwell passed out the new set to any of his female acquaintances? "There was not a sign that anyone had tried to break into the house," Barnes says. "The man who killed Elwell was a man with another key to the house, in my opinion, though I do not know where he could have got it. Elwell did not know there was anyone in the house besides himself. He was a very sensitive man and did not let anybody know of the false hair and teeth, which he had removed. Find the man with the other key and you will have solved the mystery."

## SATURDAY, JUNE 19, 1920

Now it turns out that John Isdale, who claimed to have seen Elwell enter his house at 3:45 a.m. on June 11, isn't Elwell's neighbor after all; his uncle is, and Isdale was merely spending the night there. He didn't even know Elwell and can't be sure he was the man he saw. But if *someone* did enter Elwell's house at 3:45 a.m., and someone else drove that person there, why hasn't either one stepped forward?

Reached at the Manhattan Club, DA Swann tells reporters, "The police and district attorney have no more legal evidence as to who committed the crime or whether it was committed by a man or a woman than we had five minutes after the crime was committed."

## SUNDAY, JUNE 20, 1920

Edwin Rhodes, Elwell's chauffeur at the time of his death, shares a whopper of a story with investigators: While still in Palm Beach shortly before he died, Elwell broke it off with a married woman because, he told her, her husband had suspected they were having an affair and threatened him with bodily harm. Rhodes, who witnessed the scene as it unfolded in a garage, says the women charged Elwell with inventing an excuse to break off their relationship and "became hysterical in her reproaches in the presence of garage employees." Authorities refuse to say whether Rhodes remembered the names of the man and woman involved.

Rhodes suspects Elwell picked up a woman on the street on the way home from the New Amsterdam and took her back with him. "Elwell often would see a woman on the street, order me to stop the car and take her in. He did not care whether he knew her or not," Rhodes says. If rebuffed, Elwell would explain that it was a mistake in identity. Asked if he has any guess as to who killed Elwell and why, Rhodes replies, "It seems as though it was a woman, because Mr. Elwell traveled with so many, married and single, that would be most likely."

## Monday, June 21, 1920

Investigators say they are now looking for an "unwritten law" avenger, meaning a killer enraged that Elwell was carrying on with his wife, daughter, girlfriend, whatever. "I believe that it was an unwritten law murderer, but I am anxious to have it cleared up," Swann says. Incredibly, Swann says that if it was some man protecting a woman's honor, he'd be totally cool with that. "If it was a row over money, or anything of that kind, I want to see the murderer go to the chair. While I am ready to go the limit to see the murderer caught, I probably would be as anxious as anybody to see the man freed if it was an unwritten law case, in which Elwell was punished for ruining a wife or daughter."

## Tuesday, June 22, 1920

Mystery solved! Well, not *the* mystery, but *a* mystery. Elly Hope Anderson admits to being the "Woman in Black" who dined and danced with Victor von Schlegell on the roof of the Ritz-Carlton the night before Elwell's murder. Described in the press as "a pretty girl of a distinctly Norse type, tall, blonde and with a richly modulated contralto voice," the twenty-two-year-old Anderson says, "Of course I was with [von Schlegell] in the evening, and I had breakfast with him the following morning. He asked me to do that because Friday was to be my last morning in New York—I was to leave then for my home in Minneapolis—and I consented because we had been good friends." Anderson calls her relationship with von Schlegell "friendly," hardly an accurate characterization.

She confirms von Schlegell's account of the night of the tenth; the encounter with Elwell and his companions was "entirely accidental." Von Schlegell, knowing it was her last night in the city, phoned her earlier in the day and invited her to dinner at the restaurant of her choice. She picked the Ritz-Carlton. Von Schlegell interacted twice that night with Elwell, both times "brief, casual, and apparently without any ill feeling on either side." They first crossed paths at the checkout room; von Schlegell approached the room to check their coats just as Elwell was leaving. "I don't recall who spoke first, but I remember that both men smiled and that Mr. von Schlegell waved his hand." After taking the elevator upstairs, she and von Schlegell discovered they were two tables away from the Elwell party.

"As Mr. von Schlegell and I sat down, he remarked with a laugh that he seemed unable to keep away from Viola Kraus, even though the law had given him the privilege. . . . Of course he didn't mean anything by that remark. It was just a joke. He spoke about her several times, but always with the utmost good humor."

The second encounter happened on the dance floor, when they almost collided with Elwell and Kraus. Elwell and von Schlegell smiled at each other again, she says. "I think I saw Mr. von Schlegell smile at Miss Kraus too, but I could not be certain. I know she didn't respond, because I remember she was decidedly expressionless, sort of wooden faced, every time I caught sight of her during the evening."

## WEDNESDAY, JUNE 23, 1920

June is shaping up as a miserable month for William H. Pendleton. The phone company reports that three calls were placed from the Elwell residence on the morning of June 11: one at 4:39 a.m. (to Pendleton), one at 6:09 (to Elwell's brother, Walter), and one at 6:16 (to an S. A. Varling, who didn't even know Elwell). Turns out all three are wrong. But then Margaret Entler, another telephone operator, reports trying to put two different calls through from the Elwell residence to Pendleton, at 1:45 and 2:30 a.m., though nobody picked up. Entler can't recall if the caller was male or female but didn't notice any agitation in the voice. Preposterous! says Pendleton. The telephone in his house is located in the bedroom between his bed and his wife's, and if the phone had rung at that time of the morning both would have been startled awake. It didn't, and they weren't, he says. He hasn't a clue why Elwell would even try to call him at that hour of the morning.

Cabdriver Edger Walters tells authorities he drove Elwell home from a point near the New Amsterdam shortly *after* 2 a.m.; his account is precise enough to include the detail that Elwell instructed him to stop en route to pick up a copy of the *Morning Telegraph* at a newsstand on Sixty-sixth and Broadway (a copy of which was found in Elwell's bedroom after the murder). Walters even recalls mistaking the fare's destination for 204 West Seventieth Street but was corrected when the passenger told him to keep driving until he reached 244. Walters claimed to have recognized Elwell post facto from photos in the newspaper. The guy was a real skinflint, Walters says, tipping a dime on a sixty-cent fare. Sounds like Elwell all right. Walters is certain his fare wore a business suit, but Elwell was wearing a dress suit that night, which may or may not be a minor misidentification, because really, who can tell the difference? Police, however, make a huge deal out of the discrepancy.

## Thursday, June 24, 1920

Asked if authorities have narrowed down the list of suspects now that the investigation is in its thirteenth day, ADA Alfred Talley responds, "It has not been narrowed down at all. We are trying everything that presents itself."

## Friday, June 26, 1920

"ALL ELWELL CLUES CENTRE ON A MAN; ARREST EXPECTED"
*New York Times* headline, June 26, 1920

False alarm.

The *Times* does report that the DA's office is running down "fresh evidence involving a man who has been under suspicion for several days." The suspect, whom investigators refuse to identify, is described as both a friend and business associate of Elwell's, but someone who had admitted to keeping his distance from the murdered man of late because of Elwell's increasingly wild lifestyle.

Who could that be? William Pendleton has already told authorities exactly that. Newspapers are clearly fingering Pendleton as the killer, pointing out that Elwell's former racing partner has a habit of contradicting testimony by other witnesses. The papers are reporting that Elwell was anxious to discuss some matter of importance with the suspect shortly before his death, which the "flabbergasted" Pendleton again denies.

At least the police and DA's office are working together—not. While the DA's office had been questioning witnesses about a missing set of keys for weeks, the police had marked them as evidence and stashed them at police headquarters.

"I only found out today that the third set of keys were found on the day of the murder on a mantelpiece in Elwell's bedroom," Dooling says.

One other *very* interesting development today: Word surfaces of an exchange of letters more than eight years earlier between Elwell and Charles C. Whaley, cousin of W. Gibbs Whaley, Helen Elwell's attorney. Helen and Charles were bridge partners, at the very least, and according to Gibbs, Joseph Elwell called up Charles and lobbed accusations so scurrilous that Whaley hung up on him. Elwell then sent Charles an "abusive" letter, suggesting the two meet at the offices of Elwell's attorneys; Charles replied that Elwell's missive was "untruthful and impertinent" and that he would be happy to meet with him anytime on neutral grounds, concluding that "vituperation or abuse over the phone is simply the act of a coward." While this might strike some as an act of jealousy, Elwell was already contemplating divorce and on the prowl for evidence against his estranged wife.

Asked to comment, Helen Elwell says, "That letter from Mr. Whaley had not one word of threat in it, and it is ridiculous to think it had any bearing on the case."

Mrs. Elwell has barely figured at all in the investigation, given their longtime estrangement, but that doesn't mean she doesn't have a theory on who did away with her husband. Probably not a woman, she says, because Elwell always found a way to charm them when they became angry at him. More likely the result of a gambling dispute. "Personally, I believe that Mr. Elwell's house in Seventieth Street was nothing short of a gambling den."

## SUNDAY, JUNE 27, 1920

Pendleton, described by the *New York Times* as a "good-humored man of burly build with a ruddy complexion and white mustache," hurries into town from Saratoga Springs to clear his name, even calling a press conference. "If the whole thing were not so serious it would be the damnedest joke I ever saw," he says.

Swann eventually clears Pendleton, saying, "There is no suspect in the Elwell murder case. This statement in the newspapers is a grave injustice to the man referred to by them, against whom we have no legal evidence to justify the publication." However, a week later, he calls a press conference himself to announce that Pendleton is under suspicion again because of "contradictions" that have popped up in his testimony regarding his whereabouts on June 10 and June 11, which turn out not to be contradictions at all but rather inaccurate testimony extracted by ADA John Dooling.

If it seems like every single person ever identified as a possible suspect has been cleared by the DA, it's because they have.

## MONDAY, JUNE 28, 1920

Was Joseph Elwell involved in illicit whiskey transactions amounting to huge sums of money immediately before his death (context: the Volstead Act, aka Prohibition, went into effect on January 17, 1920)? An unidentified bloke claims to have it on good authority (a German wholesale liquor dealer) that Elwell wrote out a check for $12,700 worth of alcohol. According to this story, the liquor has already been delivered to one of Elwell's social clubs (read: the Studio Club), and the wholesaler was miffed to discover the check was canceled upon Elwell's death. Maybe Elwell was having trouble covering the cost of the transaction and was gunned down by a "messenger" sent to collect? Swann, though desperate for a break in the case, is skeptical. On the other hand, "case closed" sure would look good on his résumé.

Finally, Swann reveals the identity of the person Elwell spoke to by phone at 2:30 a.m. on the day of his murder—sort of: Miss Wilson. Gee, thanks. Miss Wilson is simply a name Viola Kraus adopted in dealing with Elwell's employees, and everyone having anything to do with the case knows it. But he refuses to comment on what Miss Wilson/Kraus and Elwell discussed, saying, "It did not amount to anything."

How's the case looking? "We have got a thousand and one collateral details, but on the main issue the evidence is entirely devoid of any fact that would justify us in accusing any man or any woman," Swann says. "All of our search and that of the police had failed to find anyone who saw the murderer go in or go out, and if this was a murder, the murderer has kept his own counsel."

## WEDNESDAY, JUNE 30, 1921

Remember that crazy story about Elwell buying $12,700 worth of bootleg whiskey? All "a dream," according to James Shevlin, federal supervising Prohibition agent. After spending over twenty-four hours investigating the allegation, Shevlin concludes there's no evidence tying Elwell to illicit liquor traffic.

"When I began the investigation of this story, I instructed my men to run down every angle of it. They reported today that not one feature of the report had been found to be true. I am satisfied the entire story is a dream."

## THURSDAY, JULY 1, 1920

Remember that crazy story about Elwell being involved in the bootlegging business? All true, according to Shevlin, who's now saying Elwell was involved in a vast conspiracy to deliver liquor to his friends and that "a number of prominent men apparently have been supplied with liquor by the bootlegging system in which Elwell took part."

According to the *New York Times*: "Federal agents believe that they will uncover one of the most extensive bootlegging organizations which has been exposed since the prohibition amendment went into effect" (which admittedly was just five months earlier, so maybe a little premature to be bragging about it).

William Barnes, Elwell's secretary, and a number of other people interviewed by authorities had all previously denied any knowledge of the murdered man's involvement in bootlegging, but one man—unidentified in press reports—finally started to squeal, revealing everything he knew about Elwell's involvement in supplying alcohol to wealthy men and their social clubs. Might any of this had anything to do with Elwell's murder?

Swann could only hope.

Now that we've met the Woman in Black and the Woman in Gray, time to introduce the Woman in White: New York socialite Josephine Wilmerding, who, if Annie Kane, Elwell's previous housekeeper, can be believed, which is in no way a guarantee, once threatened to kill "Miss Wilson"/Kraus unless she stopped seeing Elwell.

## Friday, July 2, 1920

Another round of questioning with Kraus, still being identified by Swann as Miss Wilson. The press is playing a game with him, daring him to out Miss Wilson publicly.

"What is her real name?" he is asked.

"Well, she was known to Elwell's employees and has been generally known in this case as Miss Wilson."

Kane also alleged that Wilson/Kraus once threatened to kill Elwell if he deserted her for Wilmerding. After the interrogation, Swann issues a statement saying Wilson/Kraus "had not been deserted by Elwell, and did not feel fear that she would be deserted by Elwell; that she was until recently a married woman, and that he had never proposed marriage to her, and the subject had never been suggested or discussed." According to Swann, Wilson/Kraus insisted she never had "any controversy or disagreement with any other woman regarding Mr. Elwell."

While all of this is going on, a war is brewing between Swann's office and federal Prohibition agents, who say that from here on in, they want nothing to do with Swann's team as they investigate Elwell's alleged involvement in the bootlegging ring. August Hasenflug, special counsel to Prohibition agent James Shelvin, has compiled a list of prominent men alleged to have received bootlegged alcohol through Elwell and his associates, including one big shot who has held both state and city offices.

According to Assistant Supervising Prohibition Agent John B. Quigley, ADA Alfred Talley was supposed to telephone two of his agents a day earlier to discuss important information the DA had obtained relevant to the probe. However, Talley blew the agents off. One of the agents then said, "I'm not going to waste any more time with the district attorney's office. We have conferred with them several times without obtaining any important results, and I'm tired of going up there to be filled up with hot air."

Informed of those remarks, ADA John Dooling replies, "This office is not interested in the work of the prohibition enforcement division of the government in its hunt for violators of the Volstead Act. Our only interest is in running down the murderers of Elwell."

## FRIDAY, JULY 9, 1920

Remember that crazy story about Elwell being a bootlegger? Today federal agents seize four cases of whiskey from the home of H. H. Porter, president of the American Water Works, who claims to have bought the whiskey from William H. Barnes, Elwell's secretary, who has denied any knowledge of any bootlegging operations Elwell may have been involved in. Turns out Barnes himself was most definitely involved in the bootlegging operation, having received more than $4,000 worth of liquor as steward of the Studio Club.

Asked if any evidence has surfaced tying Elwell to the conspiracy, Hasenflug responds, "I am not prepared to discuss that matter at this time. Our agents are working on this case, and with today's developments they will be busy for several days running down new leads. Our investigation has only just begun."

## FRIDAY, APRIL 1, 1921

Swann, fed up with criticism over his failure to crack the case—and allegations that he is pussyfooting around certain people of wealth and privilege—hands the reins over to former New York governor Charles S. Whitman, who agrees to review the evidence and render an opinion. Andrew Macreary, attorney for Elwell's brother and mother, calls reports that the family was behind this development "absolutely false." The family believes that investigators have done "everything in their power to solve the case," Macreary says.

"I don't think this case is ever likely to be solved," he says.

W. Gibbs Whaley, attorney for Elwell's widow, says she is "perfectly indifferent" to the reopening of the case.

The irrefutable bottom line: Not a single clue of importance has been found since the day of the murder ten months ago.

But then a twenty-three-year-old, five-foot-seven, curly-black-haired native of Bridgeport, Connecticut, goes and gets himself arrested in Buffalo on an outstanding forgery charge, which, for a brief moment at least, changes everything.

## WEDNESDAY, APRIL 6, 1921

Picked up by Buffalo police on his way to a movie with his wife, Roy Harris claims he and William "Big Bill" Dunkin were hired by a woman known to them only as Mrs. Fairchild to execute Elwell for $500 up front and an additional $4,500 apiece once the deed was done. Harris's story, as it unfolds over the ensuing days, is this, more or less, although it changes daily:

On June 9, 1920, he and Duncan are approached by Jerry, a chauffeur.

"Do you fellows want to make some easy money?" Jerry asks.

"You know me, Jerry," Bill replies. "How much money is there in it?"

Jerry points to a woman seated in a limo across the street, parked in front of the York Hotel.

"You can see for yourself what it will amount to," he says. "She owns that car. Come over and meet her."

So they do. The woman, blonde, between thirty and thirty-five, about five feet six and 135 pounds, is covered in diamonds: a large ruby lavaliere on her neck and a half dozen rings on her fingers.

"She said she had a fellow she wanted to knock off, and said she wanted to dope the whole thing out so she could let us know when the job could be done," Harris says.

The next night, June 10, they meet again. "I think we are going to get a certain man right," Fairchild says. She tells them she has a guy tailing her target; he won't be home that night, so they have to postpone the hit until the following day. She reaches into her hat bag and pulls out two rolls of bills, each bound with a rubber band.

"This party I told you about wronged me, and I'm going to get him if it costs all I have, and you fellows are going to help me," Fairchild says. "There's $450 in each of these bundles. When you put this job over for me, there will be $5,000 in it for both of you."

"Who is the bird?" Big Bill asks.

"Did you ever hear tell of Joe Elwell?" she says.

"Is that the fella that owns the racehorses?" Duncan asks. "He's kind of a sport, isn't he?"

"That is who it is," Fairchild answers.

On June 11, they rendezvous at 11:30 p.m., grab a bite to eat. At about 12:45 a.m. on June 12—a not insignificant detail, since the murder occurred on the morning of the eleventh—Harris and Duncan watch as Fairchild enters the Elwell house, unlocking the front door with a key. Harris and Big Bill follow. Now Harris is having second thoughts.

"I don't want to kill anyone," he tells Big Bill.

"We won't have to get as far as Elwell's house for a murder if you begin acting in that way."

Harris gets the message.

Fairchild splits; they make plans to rendezvous later. Hours pass. At some point Duncan tells Harris to hide out in the rear of the hallway, beneath the stairs. He hands him a .32; Duncan himself is packing a .45; he calls it his "little horse pistol." The front door rattles again. It opens. A man walks into the reception room, where Duncan is still hiding. It's Elwell. He turns on the lights, turns around, climbs the stairs, right above where Harris is hiding. Twenty or so minutes later, the phone rings. The man comes down the stairs to answer it, still wearing the same clothes he was when he walked in. He speaks, but too softly for Harris to hear, except for "All right. I'll be there." Heads back upstairs, then back downstairs. All Harris can see now, he says, is his slippers. Elwell walks over to the vestibule door, opens it, peers outside, shuts it, returns to the reception room.

About fifteen minutes later, "Bam." Duncan fires the fatal shot.

When Fairchild and Jerry blow off the rendezvous, Duncan tells Harris, "I've got two bullets left in my horse pistol for that Fairchild chicken and her dressed-up chauffeur."

Harris claims he recognizes Fairchild from her photo in the papers, but he won't identify her publicly.

As incredible as it seems, Buffalo authorities buy it.

"We thought he was a drug addict when he first blurted out this connection with the killing, but he hasn't changed his story in the slightest," says Guy B. Moore, DA of Erie County. "He has, however, added to it from time to time, but these additions have served to convince us all the more that the fellow is telling the truth."

Detective Sergeant Henry Oswald of the NYPD, not so much.

"There are ridiculous discrepancies in his story," he says.

Most glaringly, Harris insists the murder occurred on the morning of June 12, not June 11. He even doubles down on this when challenged. Harris says Elwell was wearing slippers; in fact, he was barefoot. Harris says he and Duncan both smoked Pall Mall cigarettes inside the house; the only cigarette stubs police found were up in Elwell's bedroom and the two in the reception room, one Elwell's custom brand and the other a Camel. Harris insists the reception room was to the left of the hallway as you enter the house; in fact, it was on the right. Furniture Harris claims was in the reception room wasn't. The floor was covered by a rug, he says; it wasn't.

After a two-hour interview, Dr. James W. Putnam, the alienist who examined Leon Czolgosz shortly after he gunned down President McKinley in 1901, declares Harris of sound mind.

"In a general way," Putnam says, "I would say that Harris isn't lying about his part in the murder of Elwell, but I wouldn't say that he didn't lie when he declared to me that the other fellow did the shooting. He emphasized it enough to indicate that he wanted the police to believe he didn't do the actual shooting. It does not matter so much whether he is lying about the details. The discrepancy in his story about the interior of the Elwell house wouldn't necessarily indicate that he is lying. It does not prove that he was not there, in my opinion."

## SUNDAY, APRIL 10, 1921

Roy Harris was lying. He repudiates the entire story and says he confessed hoping that he would be put to death to spare his wife any further aggravation over him.

Oswald performed some nifty police work, trapping Harris into confirming a statement by his wife, Jessie, that she was with him throughout the night of June 10 and the morning of June 12. Jessie had recalled purchasing a pair of black silk socks for her husband on his birthday, June 13, which they celebrated with a party at their home.

"Didn't you say your wife was with her mother in St. Catharines on the day of the murder?" Oswald asks Harris.

"Why don't you tell him the truth, Jessie?" Harris says. "You know you were in Canada at the time Elwell was killed."

"I would rather have you tell your story again of where I was," she replies. "You seem to be able to remember things that happened at that time much better than I do."

"Roy, what is your birthday?" Oswald asks.

"June 13."

"Did you receive a present on your last birthday?"

"Why, yes. I received a new pair of silk socks from my wife."

"Who delivered them to you?"

"Why, my wife did."

"Where did she give them to you?"

"Well, I see it's all up," Harris says. "You've got me. She told you the truth when she said she was with me all of the evening and the night of the Elwell murder. There's no use of my sticking to that story now. I might as well tell you that I was not at Elwell's house at any time on the night he was killed."

Ex-governor Charles S. Whitman, who has taken over the investigation, declares, "I never believed Harris's confession." He was, after all, a politician.

## WHODUNNIT?

So who did kill Joseph Bowne Elwell? Thanks to a stunningly ineffectual investigation by New York authorities, who can say?

Jonathan Goodman, author of *The Slaying of Joseph Bowne Elwell*, was convinced Elwell was "slain by, or in obedience to the order of, Walter Lewisohn." Goodman argues that Lewisohn was mentally unstable, and he's right about that: In May 1924, a psychiatrist at Bellevue Hospital diagnosed him with incurable chronic delusional insanity, and he was institutionalized at Blythewood Sanitarium, where he remained until his death in 1938. Goodman believed Lewisohn's insanity was inflamed by his obsession with a cabaret dancer named Leonara Hughes and his fear that Elwell, also said to be bewitched by Hughes, would snap her up. Goodman points out that Elwell was renting his house from an attorney named Bernard Sandler, whom Lewisohn had introduced him to and who most certainly would have had a key to the house, lock changes or not. Sometime after 1920, Sandler—hardly the kind of prominent lawyer Lewisohn could afford to hire—was in fact hired by the banker, and in 1924 he told the *Times* he was thinking of asking for the Elwell case to be reopened so that "Miss Viola Kraus could be cleared absolutely" (though Swann seemed to do a pretty nifty job of that in 1920).

It's a theory. No smoking gun implicates Lewisohn, or anyone else for that matter. John Isdale's testimony was intriguing: He claimed to have seen a sports car pull up to the Elwell residence at 3:45 a.m. on June 11 and a man he presumed to be Elwell step out of the car and into the house, waving to the man behind the wheel as he did so. Subsequently, it was revealed that Isdale didn't know Elwell from a hole in the wall and could have been mistaken about the identification. And authorities were convinced Elwell was already home, taking Viola Kraus's telephone call over an hour earlier. Yet Isdale had no ostensible reason for fibbing. So if not Elwell, who? The killer? Is that why neither the driver nor the man who exited the car ever stepped forward? But why would a killer drive up to his victim's house at 3:45 a.m. in a thunderous sports car almost certain to call attention to itself?

Famed mystery writer S. S. Van Dine based his 1926 novel, *The Benson Murder Case*, his first featuring gumshoe Philo Vance, on Elwell's slaying; William Powell starred as Vance in the 1930 film adaptation. We're not telling how Van Dine solved the mystery.

Almost certainly, we'll never know who killed Joseph Bowne Elwell. All we can say for certain is that for a man who barreled his way through life with very little regard to the damage left in his wake, the luck of the draw finally ran out.

7

# The Sailor, the Baker, the Westchester Head Shaker

*Westchester County*

Behold the Hostess Cupcake: a spongy, dome-shaped mound of devil's food cake stuffed with sweet vanilla cream and topped with shiny ganache frosting and a white curlicue of icing. History doesn't tell us who invented the Hostess Cupcake, but we do know it first rolled off retail shelves—minus the cream filling, looped icing, and Hostess name—in May 1919 (eleven years before Jimmy Dewar created the Hostess Twinkie) at a cost of five cents for a pack of two. These were the first snack cakes ever produced by the Continental Baking Company, formerly the Ward Baking Company, founded in 1849 by Irish immigrant Hugh Ward when he opened a shop on the Lower East Side of Manhattan. But it was Hugh's son, Robert B. Ward, a dour-looking, dark-haired fellow with a formidable mustache, who earns kudos for building it into the largest baking company in the nation by the time of his death in 1919. At the time, Robert Ward's estate was valued at $5 million, despite the loss of $1.5 million from his lunkheaded investment in the "outlaw" Federal League of Base Ball Clubs and numerous controversies, among them allegations that its Tip-Top bread contained over 60 percent mineral matter, including plaster of paris.

But take a big enough bite into the history of the Ward baking empire and you'll find something far darker than all that: On May 16, 1922, Walter Ward, son of company president George Ward, shot and killed a nineteen-year-old penniless drifter by the name of Clarence Peters. Walter Ward confessed to the killing, but twice was absolved of any responsibility, once in criminal court and once in civil. His bizarre explanation was that Peters was running a three-man blackmail ring extorting money from him for reasons he refused to reveal even in a court of law—and that remain a mystery to this day. Peters, Ward insisted, pulled a pistol on him and was gunned down in an exchange of fire in self-defense in the early-morning hours on a lonely road in northern Westchester County, a New York City suburb.

Ward's story, riddled with implausibility, led authorities on a far-reaching, prolonged investigation that wound up involving an assortment of Runyonesque characters, including gumshoes, gangsters, male prostitutes, vaudevillians, a criminal attorney nicknamed both Slippery Bill and the Great Mouthpiece of the Underworld, and a press agent known as Jimmy the Rat.

After reviewing all the evidence, New York State Attorney General Carl Sherman commented, "A conclusion of justifiable homicide is here entirely lacking."

Yet Walter Ward wound up walking away a free man, while Clarence Peters didn't get to walk away at all.

## The Victim

It's hard to imagine two men with more disparate backgrounds than Clarence Melvin Peters and Walter Stevenson Ward.

"Here were two men, as far apart socially, financially, mentally, geographically, as two men can be who speak the same language and inhabit the same land," the *New York Daily News* reported on June 10, 1923. "One, the rich son of an enormously wealthy man, college bred, with a high station in the business world, well married, father of a family, a highflier in the world of sport and in his own social circle. The other, a son of poor parents, a ne'er-do-well, uneducated, mentally deficient, associate of morons like himself, a boy in years, without a trade or calling, hardly acquainted with the appearance of a twenty-dollar bill."

Still, something set Peters and Ward on a collision course that ended in Peters's death early on the morning of May 16, 1922.

Peters was born on March 24, 1903, in Haverhill, Massachusetts, the eldest son of Elbridge Oliver Peters and Inez Capitola Hardy. Haverhill, located about thirty-five miles north of Boston, was once known as Queen Slipper City, a nod to the fact that one-tenth of all the shoes produced in the United States were manufactured there. Haverhill boasts (if that's the right word) two other claims to fame: one, as the setting for the 1916 Leyden riot, triggered when the city's mayor refused to allow City Hall to host a lecture on the appropriation of public funds for parochial schools, and two, as ground zero for the first known outbreak, in 1926, of rat-bite fever (hence, its other unofficial name: Haverhill fever).

Crime scene
PHOTO COURTESY OF THE WESTCHESTER COUNTY ARCHIVES

Peters was no choirboy. He dropped out of school at the age of fourteen. Between 1918 and 1921, he shuffled in and out of reform schools thanks to an apparently uncontrollable urge to steal objects of all shapes and sizes. The guy never seemed to have a penny in his pocket. In August 1919, he joined the US Navy, serving as an apprentice seaman for three months before a dishonorable discharge for—what else?—stealing. Back home, he pursued a series of odd jobs in between more arrests and more trips to reform schools. Unable to find work, he left Haverhill again in late April 1922 and promptly was arrested in Milford, New Hampshire, reportedly mistaken for a robbery suspect by police, who then released him and told him to beat it out of town.

Next, Peters traveled to Parris Island, South Carolina, hoping to enlist in the Marine Corps. But Peters wasn't a good enough man for the few good men, and on May 12, the Marines sent him packing upon discovering his dishonorable discharge from the navy. The recruitment center covered transportation costs for rejected aspirants as far as Philadelphia, so two days later, Peters hopped on a train and headed north, first to Philly and then to New York, arriving at Pennsylvania Station at 4:20 p.m. on May 15, 1922, just hours before he was gunned down by Walter Ward.

## The Perp

"Wine, women, horses, cards, dice and song had an irresistible attraction for Walter S. Ward," the *Daily News* reported. Ward was born on September 28, 1891, in Pittsburgh, Pennsylvania, the eldest son of George Summerville Ward and Jessie Robertson More. His mother passed away when Ward was twenty-three; his father remarried four years later. Ward was born into fabulous wealth and privilege, and by 1922, the Ward Baking Company, run by George Ward, was worth nearly $35 million, thanks to its annual production of four hundred million loaves of bread and twenty different varieties of cakes. Nepo babies Walt and Ralph, his brother, had both been awarded prestige positions: Walt, who had skipped out on the University of Pennsylvania's Wharton School after two years, was named vice president, chief purchasing agent, and head of both the New Rochelle office and the Bronx Equipment Company.

In 1915, Walter Ward married Beryl Curtis, daughter of a rich lumber merchant, and within a couple of years they had moved into a house in New

Walter and Beryl Ward leaving courthouse
PHOTO COURTESY OF JUSTIN PEAVEY

Rochelle's exclusive Sutton Manor. Daughter Betty was born in 1918, son Willard two years later. Ward was appointed chairman of the New Rochelle Board of Police Commissioners, and he and Police Chief Frank Cody became such good buddies that Cody gifted him with two revolvers: a .38-caliber automatic pistol and a prewar blue-barreled .32 that had been seized from a prisoner.

Ward couldn't compete with Peters's criminal history, but he wasn't winning any Boy Scout medals either. He was a notorious drinker, gambler, and philanderer who would disappear for days without telling anyone where he was. In the summer of 1921, he subleased a flat in the Poinciana Apartments in New York City, claiming he was a bachelor who worked in the auto industry and needed a temporary place to stay in the city. He hosted wild, late-night parties and entertained more women than any of the building staff could keep track of. "I never saw a man have so many different women," Edgar Huggins, the elevator operator, would later remember. "He brought as many as half a dozen there in a day."

"It wasn't just a procession, it was a parade," the building's porter told reporters.

That same summer, Beryl and their children vacationed in Canada, but Ward begged off, saying he had business to attend to.

Early in 1922, Ralph Ward noticed that his brother was acting strangely. He took out a $20,000 loan from the Corn Exchange Bank in New York, leveraging company stock as collateral. Ralph chipped in by putting up one hundred shares of his own; Walter refused to explain why he was so desperate for cash, but Ralph knew his brother was betting heavily on the horses. In early April, unable to pay back the loan, Walter authorized the sale of most of the collateral stock, plus some of Ralph's. Around this same time, Walter cabled his father, who was touring Europe with his second wife, Donna, asking for nearly $40,000; George replied that Walter would have to wait until he returned to New York on May 16 to discuss.

On April 22, 1922, Beryl notified Ward's colleague on the New Rochelle Board of Police Commissioners, Palmer F. Tubbs, a Ward Baking Company employee, that her husband hadn't been seen or heard from in weeks, and while he had pulled this kind of stunt multiple times before, this time she was worried. Tubbs dispatched Police Lieutenant John McGowan to the Bowie racetrack near Baltimore, and sure enough McGowan found him placing bets at the $50,000-minimum window. McGowan, a mere policeman, was afraid to approach Ward, so instead he shadowed him to the train station, where Ward departed for Washington, DC. Finally, Ralph managed to drag Walter back to New York.

On May 15, Walter spent the day in the office of the Ward Baking Company. When Ralph left at 5:30 p.m., Walter was still there. He phoned Beryl to tell her he wouldn't be coming home for dinner due to a business engagement. That night, Beryl hosted a card party at their home; Ward was supposed to attend but didn't walk in the front door until 4:30 a.m. or so the following morning.

Sometime between the phone call and his return home, Ward shot and killed Clarence Peters.

### The Body of an American

At about 7:40 a.m. on May 16, 1922, a beautiful, bone-dry Monday in the northern suburbs of New York City, a team of linemen from the Westchester Light Company happened upon the corpse of an unidentified young man on their way to a job along the Kensico Reservoir in North Castle. The man, wearing a buttoned-up coat and a cap that had been partially jarred loose from his head, lay on his back, his eyes half open.

Summoned to the scene, New York state troopers Harry Green and Ralph Collins surmised that the man had been shot in the chest, just to the right of his heart. They spotted one set of tire tracks in the gravelly road not far from the body and an empty .38 Savage automatic shell sixteen feet away. No signs of a struggle, no revolver, no bullet, no trace of blood. Emptying out the man's pockets, they found $1.32 in loose change, two dice, four cufflinks, a tiepin, a deck of playing cards, a pipe, a box of matches, a cigarette case, a pack of Chesterfield cigarettes, a broken comb, and two handkerchiefs, one embroidered with two lavender pansies. What they didn't find was any identification.

Westchester County coroner Edward Fitzgerald estimated the time of murder between 3:00 and 4:00 a.m. But not everyone agreed on where the shooting had taken place: Fitzgerald and state trooper Lieutenant Eugene Roberts both believed the shooting had taken place where the body was found, while Green, citing the absence of any indication of a struggle, dissented.

Dr. John Black's autopsy concluded that the victim had been shot at close range at a downward angle, with the bullet entering just above the heart and exiting near the spine of his lower back. The downward angle, Fitzgerald said, led him to believe "a person standing in an automobile fired the shot, which would give the range to cover the route of the bullet. The fact that no revolver was found or any signs of a struggle near the body also confirms my theory to some extent."

Because the man's underwear was tagged "US Navy," authorities reached out to Naval Intelligence, which matched the fingerprints to those of Clarence Peters.

On Friday, May 19, Westchester County's Sheriff George J. Werner and District Attorney Frederick E. Weeks agreed to meet privately in the county courthouse in White Plains with Allan R. Campbell, a Harvard Law School grad with deep connections to the Westchester County Democratic Party. Campbell stunned both men with the revelation that he was representing a client who had murdered a man in self-defense. And not just any client, but a fabulously wealthy one: the son of the owner of the largest baking company in America: Walter Ward.

Ward, Campbell said, would surrender to authorities in three days.

PHOTO COURTESY OF THE *NEW YORK DAILY NEWS*

On March 22, Ward arrived at the courthouse with his lawyers and a 331-word statement drafted, it would turn out, at Werner's request, explaining—sort of—his involvement in Peters's death. The statement went something like this: A blackmail ring involving Clarence Peters and two other men, known to him as Charlie Ross and Jack, had been extorting thousands of dollars from him over the previous six weeks. The blackmailers had threatened his life and the lives of his family. Ward had already ponied up $30,000. They demanded $75,000 more (this supposedly was when Ward cabled his father asking for money and was rebuffed). Walter Ward finally put his foot down. Hoping to "temporize and put them off," he met them on the night of Monday, May 15. Peters and Ward sat in Ward's car, a Peerless coupe; Ross and Jack were in a red Stutz. Peters stuck a gun in Ward's ribs and ordered him first to start driving, then to pull over at a deserted spot above the reservoir. The Stutz parked in front of them, partially blocking Ward's car on the narrow road. When Peters ordered Ward to exit the vehicle, Ward, convinced he was about to be killed, reached for the gun. A shot went off. Ward too was packing, and returned fire, hitting Peters. Then Ross started firing. Ward returned that fire. Then the Stutz took off, leaving Ward alone with Peters's lifeless body.

The statement contained numerous claims that contradicted the findings of police at the site. Only one set of tire tracks had been found. There'd been no signs of a struggle. No blood splattering. No shattered glass from car windows. A single bullet casing had been found, but no bullets. Authorities found a bullet hole in Peters's shirt but not in his vest or jacket, suggesting, as the *New York Times* reported, "that Peters had his coat and vest off when he was shot and that he was shot at close range." According to Clarence Eckhardt, who owned a farm nearby, his farmhands were sleeping no more than two hundred yards from the site that morning, yet none of them heard even a single shot. Footprints matching Peters's shoes were deeply set, suggesting he had been standing there for some time before he was shot, contradicting Ward's assertion that he had quickly stepped out of the car with one foot on the running board and one on the ground before Ward pulled out his revolver. According to Ward, his automobile had been riddled with bullets fired by the so-called blackmailers, but no bullet holes were found in the car. Further, if Peters did in fact have a gun on him and he was shot where his body was found, what happened to the gun? And if the blackmail scheme had been going on for weeks, as Ward maintained, how could Peters have been involved, since he had just arrived in New York from Parris Island?

Following his confession, Ward was arrested on a manslaughter charge and held on $10,000 bail, which he promptly paid in $1,000 bills extracted from his pants pocket.

## What's It All About?

Ward's confession included multiple discrepancies, but even more noteworthy was what it *didn't* include: any motive for the blackmail.

Publicly at least, Werner expressed little interest in finding out, calling it "a private matter" sure to incite a scandal should newspapers find out. Instead, Werner was focused on tracking down Charlie Ross and Jack. The case, he added, "appears to have been plainly one of blackmail." So whatever Ward was selling, Werner was buying, at least publicly.

Others, not so much. Massachusetts lawyer Michael Sullivan, hired by Peters's parents, called Ward's "confession" "a blackmail yarn."

"What was the alleged blackmail threat based on?" he asked. "Where and when were the demands made?" Ward, he said, should be compelled to provide these and other details.

Reporters naturally were champing at the bit to discover the scandal behind the blackmail. Racetrack gambling? Another woman (or two or three or four)? Was Ward a "degenerate," a euphemism of the time for queer people? Or was something shifty going on at the Ward Baking Company?

As the *New York American* phrased it, "What was the strange hold that the alleged blackmailing ring seemed to have on Ward, thirty-one years old and married?"

On May 24, police learned that five weeks before the murder, around the time Ward claimed to have first been approached by the blackmailers, he had overdosed on iodine. Beryl, who discovered him thrashing about on the floor of their library, summoned a doctor, who pumped his stomach. At first it was believed to be accidental—Ward had been suffering from intense headaches—but rumors soon circulated that he was trying to end his life. Ward's doctor, Orville Schell, told reporters the overdose was accidental. "I do not know differently, and you must believe a man innocent until he is proven guilty," he said. The day after the story hit the newsstands, Ward resigned as chairman of the New Rochelle Board of Police Commissioners.

One day later, Ward's attorney Allan Campbell visited Werner's office to deliver two guns: a .38 Colt automatic revolver and a .32 Smith & Wesson pistol. Werner assembled reporters to fill them in on what he had learned:

As I understand the affair, Ward put his own gun into his pocket after he had downed Peters and then, seized with some sort of an impulse, picked up Peters's gun from the roadway and tucked that gun away also. When Ward's automatic came into my hands, it was entirely empty, although Ward's story is that he fired three cartridges.

Werner also produced the coat, vest, and shirt that Peters had been wearing at the time of his death, arguing that the coat and vest were cut so low in front that the bullet that killed Peters would not have pierced through the front of the garments even if the coat and vest had been buttoned.

"What about Ward's automobile, which was said by Ward to have been riddled in the pistol battle?" one reporter asked.

"I am not ready yet to talk about the automobile," Werner replied.

"Have you anything to show where Ward and Peters first met?"

"Not a thing."

Werner told reporters he now believed Ward had fired two shots in addition to the one that killed Peters. One empty shell had been found in Ward's car and another in the road, he said. The third was still missing.

DA Weeks also met with reporters that day, prompting this exchange:

"On the night of May 15, the night of the shooting, did anyone see Ward anywhere except along the route he describes having traversed, the main road north of White Plains, to a point six miles north, at the end of the Kensico Reservoir?" one reporter asked.

"It appears not," Weeks replied.

"Is there any inkling of the identity of the two men, Charlie Ross and Jack, said by Ward to have been with Clarence Peters?"

"Not an inkling."

"Did anybody see anything of the red Stutz car described by Mr. Ward, or did anybody catch a glimpse of the license number?"

"No, and again no."

Asked if Ward had explained privately the reasons for the blackmail, Weeks replied, "He has not."

"Do you regard it as unusual—strange—that Ward, after killing Peters, should have paused to pick up the revolver of the man he had slain?" a reporter asked.

"No, I cannot say it was."

Coroner Edward Fitzgerald announced that he was delaying the inquest "until I can get sufficient evidence to make Ward talk more freely than he has yet done. As it is now, he can stand upon his constitutional rights and decline to say anything. We are doing the best we can to check up on his story, and that's all there is to it.

"Before I accept Ward's claim of shooting in self-defense, I have to have more evidence than has been placed before me or has come to my attention so far. I say flatly that the story does not ring true. It has discordant notes."

As doubts about the veracity of Ward's explanation mounted, the grand jury advocated that Ward be arrested again, this time charged with first-degree murder. Werner obliged and brought Ward back to his office. Reporters congregated outside reported that Ward was in good spirits, smiling and laughing as he and his lawyers dined with Werner around the conference table on takeout food. When Werner and Ward made a dash for the entrance to the county jail about 120 feet away in the rain, reporters followed in pursuit. Ward slipped in the rain before regaining his footing, but when they got to the entrance, they found it locked.

"What's the matter, Mr. Ward, won't they let you in?" one reporter asked, prompting a smile from Ward.

Ward was given a private room, and the following morning he breakfasted with Werner in the sheriff's office. Then Campbell and Weeks took turns arguing before Justice Frank L. Young of the New York Supreme Court over the terms of Ward's release, with Weeks seeking $50,000 bail. "When we ask for explanation and amplification of his version of the killing, we were given to understand we could take it or leave it," Weeks said. "This case is as mysterious now as it was the morning the unidentified body was found in the lonely road near the reservoir."

Young sided with Weeks: "Whether it is a case of murder or manslaughter it is now impossible to determine satisfactorily. The only witness so far is the defendant himself, and his testimony is entitled to be considered with care."

Ralph Ward forked over the bail money later that day, doling out forty-nine $1,000 bills and two $500 bills to the court clerk.

## The Elusive Duo

Did Charlie Ross and Jack really exist? Or were they merely figments of Walter Ward's imagination? Inquiring minds wanted to know—Werner, Weeks, lawyers, reporters, cops, even private detectives hired by both sides among them. Private citizens also got in on the action, no doubt eyeing a $1,000 reward being offered by the *New York American*. Ward had described Ross as Jewish, thirty or so years old, five feet nine or ten, with wavy, light-brown hair. Jack, whom Ward labeled a dope fiend, was pasty faced, five feet ten, 160 pounds, with straight black hair.

"These persons, who rode to the rendezvous with Ward in a red Stutz, have completely erased themselves," the *New York Herald* reported on May 26. "Not a trace of them has been discoverable. No person has been found who saw them going or coming, and no record has been obtained of the red Stutz."

New York City police joined the manhunt, dropping in on well-known hangouts for blackmailers and extortionists in Manhattan.

"We tried to get Ward to amplify his descriptions of Ross and Jack," one frustrated New York City detective told reporters. "Every time we tried to ask a question, his lawyer jumped right in."

On May 27, prominent New York criminal attorney William Fallon (nicknamed the Great Mouthpiece, he had defended gangster Arnold Rothstein, accused of fixing the 1919 World Series), hired by Michael Sullivan, told Weeks he had tracked down Ross and Jack and would deliver them to the DA's office the following day. Fallon may not have been the most reliable source, given that he eventually would be indicted himself for bribing a juror. Sure enough, Fallon failed to deliver, prompting the *Daily News* to dispatch a reporter to East 178th Street in the Bronx, where a man named Nathan Rosenzweig lived with his mother, two married sisters, and a brother. Rosenzweig, it turned out, had gone by the alias Nat Ross when he and accomplice Samuel Dreyvus were arrested for blackmailing wealthy New York banker Orville Tobey, whom they threatened to expose as a degenerate.

The reporter was greeted at the door by one of Rosenzweig's sisters, who "became hysterical with anger and grief when the reporter's mission was discovered." When the *Daily News* reporter mentioned Ward's name, the sister "became purple with rage," calling Ward "a scoundrel who lures innocent boys away from their innocence." The reporter then visited a poolroom Rosenzweig frequented, where an argument with his brother, Joe, became so heated that the two of them wound up in the hoosegow. "I'll kill you or any other *News* reporter who comes near our home again," Joe Rosenzweig said. "I've got a gun in my pocket right now if you want to see it. I wouldn't hesitate to kill you right now."

Despite Fallon's characteristic grandstanding—and the volatile responses to the *News* reporter by Rosenzweig's relatives—no evidence ever surfaced linking him to the Ward-Peters affair, and a private detective for the Val O'Farrell Agency, which Fallon had enlisted for assistance, told reporters, "Truthfully, I do not think that either one of them know anything about the Ward case." O'Farrell agreed: "In my estimation, there is absolutely no connection between Charlie Ross and Jack and Ward." O'Farrell operative Harry Conners, who tracked the two men to a hotel in Boston, also told reporters that they knew nothing about Ward.

When Rosenzweig was eventually cajoled into visiting Weeks's office, the DA arranged a meeting with Ward, who insisted he had never seen the man before in his life.

Meanwhile, an ex-serviceman calling himself James C. Clark (an alias) claimed to have spent the summer of 1921 with Peters hanging out in Bryant Park, a notorious pickup spot for gay men, and sharing a room with him at a boardinghouse in Times Square. Clark's story was that Peters was whoring himself out to deep-pocketed men, including a policeman from New Rochelle. Other denizens of the park claimed to have seen Peters together with Ward.

## Rumors and Innuendo

By now, rumors were flying about Ward's sex life. He frequented men-only parties in Boston. He was seen leaving one such party with Peters. The editor of the *Boston Advertiser* claimed Ward was intimate friends with a queer Boston hotelier known for throwing wild parties. At a New York pool hall, con man Harry Bosky told detectives it was common knowledge that Ward was a degenerate and had been "shaken down" over it at least twice before.

On May 28, Christopher Ryan, a New York waiter, told authorities a mysterious young woman had offered him $500 to assassinate Ward. Ryan tried to lure the woman to a subsequent meeting so that authorities could listen in, but she bailed.

On May 30, Martha Kendall Mellen, a former vaudeville performer and waitress, revealed that she and Ward had started to have an affair in 1915, the same year he married Beryl, and that later that year he had broken into her apartment and tried to kidnap her. She claimed that she had threatened to sue Ward for $10,000 but was paid off by George Ward. According to a chiropractor by the name of Dr. Souchelle, Mellen claimed she had been raped by Ward and became pregnant with his son.

Ward was "a man absolutely without honor when it comes to women," Mellen told the *Times*.

"He always cried 'blackmail' when he was in trouble," Mellen told reporters. "Find the woman in the case, and the Ward blackmail mystery will be solved," she told a reporter for the *Los Angeles Times*.

Soon, however, another version of the story surfaced: A blackmail ring had coaxed Mellen into extorting $10,000 from Ward to cover up their affair. Ward refused to pay; she first filed suit, then dropped it once she was paid off. Reporters looking to confirm the story found that the court records had disappeared, and Mellen's lawyer had since been disbarred.

The *New York American* then reported that James Cunningham, aka Jimmy the Rat, claimed Peters was killed not by the reservoir but in Ward's house. Cunningham's story was that Ward was playing a confidence game of his own, scheming with the blackmailers to extort money from his father. Once George refused to pay up, the blackmailers, including Peters, set a trap at Walt's house, hoping to expose his role in the extortion ring to his father, but things went haywire and Ward wound up shooting Peters in the commotion. Cunningham claimed that another of the blackmailers was also shot, then rushed to a doctor in Stamford, Connecticut, for treatment. But authorities tracked down the Stamford doctor, who told them Cunningham's yarn was "utterly false." Detectives then arranged a meeting between Cunningham and Ward at the White Plains jail.

"Hey, Ward! How are you?" Cunningham said.

"What do you mean?" Ward responded. "I never met you before in my life."

When Cunningham protested that Ward simply didn't recognize him because he had grown a mustache, Ward told his attorney, "I don't know this man. Come on, let's get out of here."

Elwood Rabenold, another of Ward's high-powered attorneys, labeled Cunningham's allegations the "wild, indefensible dream of a crazy criminal."

Another story surfaced that Ward, a frequent visitor to the Empire City racetrack in Yonkers, New York, during the summer of 1921, was paying Charlie Ross and his associates a hefty fee in exchange for tips on rigged races. Ward was rolling in the dough at first, but eventually the tips stopped paying off, and when Ward tried to bail, Ross threatened to expose not just Ward's role in the illegal betting scheme but also unsavory secrets from both his past and his father's.

## ELEMENTARY, WATSON?

On June 6, the Ward case was finally presented to the grand jury. Prosecutors kept trying to force Ward's dad to testify, but George was avoiding New York State, so was beyond the reach of a subpoena. Finally, authorities charged him with conspiring with Walt to thwart justice. Ralph Ward did eventually testify—combatively—but didn't have much to say. On June 15, Ward was indicted on a charge of first-degree murder and once again arrested.

On June 24, reporters catching up with Sherlock Holmes creator Arthur Conan Doyle as he waited to board the RMS *Adriatic* for the return trip home asked for his thoughts about the Peters murder. An "ideal Sherlock mystery," Doyle called it, suggesting that authorities focus on solving the puzzle of the alleged blackmail scheme. By this time a confirmed spiritualist, Doyle added that a psychically gifted detective could crack the case under the right circumstances.

"Not through spiritualism, mind you, because I don't believe Peters has been dead long enough or was of great enough intelligence to communicate with a stranger, but through occultism or mind impressions," Doyle said. "It is possible, however, that someone very near and dear to Peters might get into communication with him and learn the whole story of his death direct from his spirit. I firmly believe this is possible."

Judge Joseph L. Morschauser, meanwhile, was focusing on less numinous matters, like a June 20 letter from Susquehanna, Pennsylvania, signed "B.T.D."

"Dear Friend: If you don't set him free, my friend, Walter S. Ward, I will shoot you dead in ten days. He is a good man. All you want is to get his money away from him."

In early July, Walter Ward, still lounging in his jail cell, received an interesting letter of his own, from a Haverhill, Massachusetts, woman claiming she had information that could save his life.

"Please act quickly," the letter concluded.

### Keeping Up with the Joneses

The author of this missive was Goldie Jones, who revealed that she had been interviewed by A. B. Monroe of the Pinkerton Detective Agency. Monroe told Jones he was working on Ward's behalf, and while Jones initially believed him, she was beginning to have second thoughts. Monroe *was* in fact a Pinkerton operative but was working for Weeks rather than Ward. Jones told Monroe that Peters had visited her and her daughter, Queenie, many times during that spring, regaling them with yarns about trips he had taken to New York City. According to Jones, Peters was leaving Haverhill for New Rochelle, where he "had a very wealthy friend." Peters did in fact leave Haverhill that spring, but for Parris Island, not New Rochelle. Goldie, a native Liverpudlian, told Peters she yearned to return home, and he promised to fund her trip with money from his friend. He'd also promised Queenie a diamond ring, Goldie said.

Soon after this, the Jones family mysteriously disappeared from Haverhill.

With no trial date set by the beginning of 1923, Ward's attorneys asked Justice Albert H. F. Seeger to dismiss the indictment. Seeger, saying the case had grown "stale," granted the request. "Killing a man in self-defense is no crime," he ruled on January 2. "The State has shown nothing to prove Peters was not killed in self-defense. It is therefore better for the State this motion is granted."

The *Daily News* erupted with anger, alleging that the Westchester County Republican Party had pulled strings, allowing Ward to get off scot-free.

"Many Westchester folk resent the implication that a rich man, or a rich man's son, can kill a man in that county and get away with it; can be indicted by a grand jury for murder and never brought to trial; can be set free by the courts solely because of a prosecutor's unexplained failure to prosecute," the *News* wrote.

## Sherman's March

About two weeks later, Inez Peters, standing outside newly elected Governor Alfred Smith's office, told reporters she had come to Albany "to plead with Governor Smith for justice, because I have read of his great devotion to his aged mother, and I felt that he would see that justice was done."

Her attorney, Fred Maginson, argued for a new jury trial, insisting that "the facts disprove every statement made on behalf of Ward. What we do know is that Walter Ward killed Clarence Peters, and he is a free man today."

Smith was convinced enough to order his staff attorneys to conduct an investigation, and in March he announced he was reopening the case. New York Attorney General Carl Sherman would lead the investigation. "I have reached the conclusion that this thing ought to be cleaned up once and for all," Smith said.

Three days later, hearings began in Albany. Sherman subpoenaed dozens of witnesses.

It surfaced during these hearings that Ward's 331-word statement had been drafted by Allan Campbell and Elwood Rabenold, but both attorneys refused to say whether Ward had approved it or how they had obtained the explanation of the shooting put forth in the statement.

When Sherman asked New Rochelle's Police Chief Frank Cody whether Ward, as Police Commissioner Board chairman, could have come to him for protection from the blackmailers, Cody replied, "He sure could, yes, sir. He was the boss. We were there to do what he told us."

Assistant Attorney General Wilbur Chambers opted to restage the shooting at the site where Peters's body was discovered. Three men who had been returning from Connecticut late on May 15 when their truck broke down, forcing them to spend the night parked a mile south of where the body was found, had told authorities they hadn't heard any gunshots. To test their testimony,

Chambers and three witnesses stood where the truck had broken down as state troopers fired twenty-one shots into the air. Only two or three were heard. But farmer Clarence Eckhardt, who lived just up the hill from the site and had also said he didn't hear any shots that night, heard all twenty-one during the restaging. Chambers told reporters he was "thoroughly convinced that the story of the shooting as related by Ward's attorneys is false from start to finish."

In late April, Sherman announced he had received a letter from Queenie Jones, who was now in England, alleging that Ward's attorneys and agents acting on their behalf "had the Jones family under their wing for a period of time at various apartments and hotels in New York City." It turned out that just after Justice Seeger declared Ward a free man, Ward's attorneys at Rabenold & Scribner had purchased tickets for Goldie Jones and her family to sail to Liverpool. The lawyers had promised to leave money with the ship's purser for their resettlement but failed to deliver. For the previous six months, after leaving Haverhill, the Joneses had surreptitiously lived in Harlem, their hundred-dollar monthly rent paid, plus a monthly stipend, by Rabenold & Scribner's Samuel Miller, who insisted under oath that he had done so "within my own discretion." Asked if he had encouraged the Joneses to move to New York, he replied, "I didn't bring them. They came with me."

Using letters the Joneses had written to friends, the *Daily News*'s Julia Harpman reported that Ward's attorneys had coached Goldie and Queenie to lie about Peters during a series of meetings held in the summer and fall of 1922. Asked if she thought Peters was a degenerate, Goldie replied no, but the attorneys coached her to say "Yes, he was—and a blackmailer too."

"They told me to say that I knew that Peters had received a letter addressed to him in care of the White Plains post office, telling about a certain millionaire who would pay to keep something quiet," Goldie said. In truth, she added, "I am sure Peters was not a blackmailer. I don't believe he even knew Ward."

That same month, Sherman received another letter, from C. V. Knightley, formerly a secretary at the Boston YMCA, who claimed that Peters and Ward were homosexually involved. Knightley said he had encountered Peters at Penn Station on the afternoon of May 15, 1922, and that Peters had asked him for $5, saying he was trying to get to New Rochelle. Knightley claimed to know how and where the murder happened: "Peters was shot at Mrs. Ward's bedroom door," he wrote, adding that Ward then dropped Peters's body by the reservoir. "No other men were present," he wrote.

In May, Sherman announced, "Without in any way indicating my belief in the guilt or innocence of Walter S. Ward, I believe that sufficient grounds exist for the submission of all available facts to a grand jury with a view toward procuring an indictment charging Walter S. Ward with such an offense as the facts would warrant.

"A conclusion of justifiable homicide," he added, "is here entirely lacking."

This time, the prosecution would be handled by Sherman himself, with the New York Supreme Court's Justice Robert Wagner presiding.

Sherman called seventy-three witnesses, including Ralph Ward, who was his usually surly self, although he did concede that he had asked his father for $90,000 for his brother; George initially agreed to cough up the money, but after learning that it was intended to pay off blackmailers, he changed his mind. George did share the entire story of the blackmail with Ralph, but Ralph refused to reveal what was said. Weeks, no longer the county DA, told the grand jury he originally believed Ward's confession, but "after I mulled it over a couple of days, why, I didn't believe it at all." Weeks further claimed that he had been "abused" by Ward's attorneys, and when he urged Campbell to come clean on the nature of the blackmail, Campbell replied, "We will not be forced either by the public or popular clamor to say what the blackmail is."

William Mundia, a twenty-five-year-old chauffeur and former inmate of the Matteawan State Hospital for the Criminally Insane, testified that he had accompanied Ward to cabarets and private parties in New York City and that he had seen Peters with Ward at Cushman's cabaret a few times in May, although his physical descriptions of both men were inaccurate. He maintained that Ward had paid him $12 to $15 dollars for unspecified "depraved practices." Mundia claimed he had agreed to meet Ward early on the morning of May 16, 1922, on a road near the reservoir, Ward having confided to him that two men named Jack Rogers and Charlie Ross initially had agreed to murder Peters but then refused, leaving Ward to do it himself. He said Ward offered him $5,000 to keep quiet, but he refused because he didn't have a bank account.

On Friday, July 27, the grand jury announced its verdict: "Walter S. Ward, you have been indicted for the crime of murder in the first degree," the court clerk read. Ward pleaded not guilty, and the trial began on September 17. On Tuesday, September 25, just seven days in, the prosecution rested. The following day, Isaac Mills, another of Ward's attorneys, announced that the defense too rested—without calling a single witness.

Mills's closing statement lasted an incredible four hours, and at one point Beryl Ward began crying and had to be revived with smelling salts. Mills described Peters as a "blackmailer by hire" who, having just arrived in New York, "hired himself out undoubtedly that evening for a few paltry dollars to serve as the gunman."

Finally, Mills asked Ward to stand, and he handed the jury a photo of Beryl with the Wards' two children.

"Do you think these are the children of a murderer?" he asked.

Mills defended Ward's refusal to reveal the nature of the blackmail, arguing, "Suppose you had gone astray. Suppose you have fallen into the hands of evil men, and they discovered something of the past which affects your character and standing? What would you do? Do you think that they ought to be allowed to throw wide the door of their closet and disclose to the public the skeleton hanging there? Of course not.

"I commit to your keeping, to your consciences, to your judgment, as men of sense and honor and decency, this man, this woman, these little children, for deliverance from this horrid persecution, unjust, and unprecedented, which has tormented them for sixteen months."

Sherman countered by arguing that Ward's refusal to present a single shred of evidence backing up the blackmail claim was proof enough that Ward was lying.

"You don't want to know the details of that secret, and neither do I, but don't you want some proof of how these alleged blackmailers operated?" he said. "Don't you want to see some of these terrible letters he says they wrote him? He simply says, 'I've been blackmailed, you've [got to accept] that as a fact.' Isn't there some evidence of the blackmail you'd like to see?

"The statute defines homicide as the killing of a human being—not a good man, a black man or a white man—not a rich man or a poor man, a villain or a hero, but a human being. And you cannot take a human life without justification, no matter who you are, without being brought to trial for it and having a jury decide whether you were justified or not."

After deliberating for three hours and taking four votes, the jury delivered its verdict on September 29, Walter Ward's thirty-second birthday:

Not guilty.

Once again, Walter Ward was a free man.

In an interview for this book, James Polchin, author of *Shadow Men: The Tangled Story of Murder, Media, and Privilege That Scandalized Jazz Age America*, said, "What actually happened is of course the million-dollar question. I have gone through all the existing records of the case (and there is much missing) and still have no concrete answer."

Polchin's best guess: Peters, on his way back to Haverhill after being booted from the Marines, hitchhiked from Philadelphia to New York, where he bumped into Ward, a complete stranger. They had sex. Ward panicked and shot Peters, leaving him in the secluded area by the reservoir. Whatever identifying papers Peters had on him, Ward absconded with, figuring Peters would be treated as a John Doe and buried in a paupers' field.

"Ward could not have imagined that Peters's underwear would lead to the military records and fingerprinting," Polchin figures. "When news of Peters's identity was made known, Ward came forward with an attorney-concocted story about blackmail. Why he came forward at all is a mystery, except that there might have been people who could have connected Peters to Ward that last night of Peters's life."

And what about Ward's blackmail story? Polchin believes Ward very well may have been targeted by blackmailers, but doubts Peters was involved:

> There is no evidence Peters was the kind of person to plan out an elaborate blackmail. A petty thief and dreamer of a better life, sure. I doubt Jack and Charlie ever existed, and certainly there was not another car pulling up along King Street with blackmailers firing at Ward. I think the blackmail may have been a separate issue, perhaps something that propelled Ward to Maryland to try to raise a lot of money at the racetrack and later ask for money from his father. I suspect that the secret behind it was much worse than anything that could be printed at the time, so the family kept it all quiet. By claiming Peters' murder as part of a blackmail scheme, Ward and his lawyers would have also squashed the threats of the blackmailers, as they would certainly not come forward amidst the media frenzy and police investigation and risk their own prosecution.

A man named Justin Peavey also has taken a special interest in this case, with good reason: a Haverhill native, Peavey learned of his relationship to Peters—his grandfather's uncle—through a genealogical message board. His grandfather's cousin posted that "Uncle Charlie" had been killed in New York State in the early 1900s and that "if Nana had a better lawyer, we'd own the Hostess Company." In an interview for this book, Peavey said the details of the murder as originally relayed to him were exaggerated, which didn't surprise him because Peters was killed years before his grandfather was born, so it was all hearsay. "The story hadn't been passed on to us by our forebears either," he said.

"My mother certainly never heard of it." Peavey started digging into the murder and even dramatized it for his thesis project in college. Like everyone else, he said, "I've never settled on anything that I felt was a reasonable explanation for the killing."

One thing Peavey is convinced of: "Walter Ward and Clarence Peters could never have met before the evening of May 15."

## THE REST OF THE STORY

In 1926, Clarence Peters's parents filed a civil suit against Walter Ward, seeking $75,000. On May 6 of that year—one week before Ward was scheduled to appear in civil court—his automobile was found abandoned in Trenton, New Jersey. Ward, who had been MIA since traveling to Baltimore on a purported business trip on May 5, was nowhere to be found. Even without Ward present, the jury was deadlocked, and the suit was dismissed. Plans for a retrial never materialized.

Five months later, newspapers reported that Beryl and Walter Ward had met secretly on multiple occasions in Tuckahoe, New York, since Ward's bizarre disappearance. Asked about this, Beryl threatened to sic a police dog on the reporter.

In January 1927, Ward finally reappeared in public, having sailed from New Orleans to his father's estate in Havana, Cuba, his new home.

In September 1927, Beryl Ward, having not laid eyes on her husband for a year and a half, took a train to Reno, Nevada, where she petitioned for a divorce that was eventually granted. "I intend to forget Walter Ward completely," she said in her last interview, with the *New York American*. "He has my best wishes, but he is out of my life forever."

"People have wondered, I am told, at my silence concerning the unfortunate events that brought me and those nearest me into nationwide attention," she added. "There have been hints that I was silenced by suppression from Walter Ward's family. That is not true. My silence was entirely voluntary. I felt too deeply and suffered too much to give it voice."

Walter Ward, who eventually remarried, passed away in 1946 in Havana at the age of fifty-three, due to pulmonary emphysema. His remains were moved to a family lot with a large monument at the Kensico Cemetery in Valhalla, New York, not far from where Clarence Peters's body had been discovered twenty-four years earlier.

# 8

# Locked and Loaded

## *New York City*

Sometime during the sixth century BCE, the prophet Daniel set out to convince Cyrus the Great, King of the Persians, that the idol Bel was a false god. Cyrus's priests had succeeded in convincing him otherwise, and when your name ends with "the Great," you probably aren't all that amenable to being told you're wrong. Still, it seemed rather obvious to Daniel, given that Bel was made out of clay and bronze.

"Do you not see how much he eats and drinks every day?" the king asked Daniel.

Indeed, every day the priests presented Bel with "twelve great measures of fine flour, and forty sheep, and six vessels of wine," and every day the food and drink disappeared, apparently consumed by this magnificent deity.

One day seventy of Cyrus's priests beseeched the king to place the usual offerings inside the temple where Bel resided and then seal off the entrance with his ring, which he did. The following morning, the food and drink were gone, the wax seal unbroken.

Surely this was proof that Bel was the real deal? Except that Daniel had surreptitiously scattered ashes over the floor of the temple after the priests had clocked out for the night, revealing footprints leading to a secret doorway through which the priests, their wives, and their children had entered during the night to consume the offerings.

This was terrible news for the priests, their wives, and their children, all of whom were put to death, but excellent news for writers of detective fiction, because Daniel had unknowingly just invented a new subgenre: the locked-room mystery, or, as it is sometimes known, the "impossible crime."

Otto Penzler, founder of The Mysterious Press and proprietor of The Mysterious Bookshop in New York City, defines the locked-room mystery as a "catch-all phrase meaning the telling of a crime that appears to be impossible. The story does not actually require a hermetically sealed chamber so much as a location with an utterly inaccessible murder victim. A bludgeoned, stabbed or strangled body in the centre of pristine snow or sand is just as baffling as a lone figure on a boat at sea or aboard a one-man plane or in the classic locked room."

Edgar Allan Poe is widely credited with having invented the locked-room mystery with "The Murders in the Rue Morgue" (1841), in which a mother and daughter are discovered brutally murdered in their apartment. The windows and doors are locked from the inside, the chimney is deemed impassable, and no loose floorboards or secret passages are discovered. However, Robert Adey, in his exhaustive bibliography *Locked Room Murders and Other Impossible Crimes*, argues that the honor actually belongs to the Irish novelist Joseph Thomas Sheridan Le Fanu, author of the 1838 story "A Passage in the Secret History of an Irish Countess." No matter; almost every major mystery writer since the beginning of time has crafted at least one locked-room mystery story of their own, including Wilkie Collins, Arthur Conan Doyle, S. S. Van Dine, John Dickson Carr (the so-called "maestro" of the locked-room mystery), Ellery Queen, Agatha Christie, and Soji Shimada. Gaston Leroux, far better known as the author of *The Phantom of the Opera*, contributed *Mystery of the Yellow Room* in 1907, Carr's nominee for the greatest locked-room murder mystery of all time.

Some 2,500 years after Daniel's exposé of the imposter Bel, a thirty-seven-year-old, soulful-looking proprietor of a laundry business in upper Manhattan with an aquiline nose; dark, piercing eyes; and a scraggly beard was discovered murdered in his business establishment, the doors and windows of which were securely locked from the inside. The man's name was Isidore Fink, and all these years later, his death remains one of the most baffling murder mysteries of all time.

## THE VICTIM

Isidore Fink was born in World War I–ravaged Eastern Europe—some say Poland, some say Russia—and immigrated to the United States in 1921, landing at Ellis Island in determined pursuit of the American dream. Fink owned the Fifth Avenue Laundry, a two-room business establishment on the ground floor of a tenement building at 4 East 132nd Street, directly across the street from a used-furniture store operated by his buddy Max Sternberg. Fink's laundry was at the southeastern tip of Harlem, an area of upper Manhattan that in 1929 was experiencing the very last gasps of the famed Harlem Renaissance.

In Isidore Fink's little corner of the world, crime was spiraling, especially holdups. Still, a man needed to earn a living, so Fink kept the laundry open late on Saturdays—until midnight—despite being fully aware of the dangers posed by such a risky decision. Fink was hardly reckless, however: He was obsessive about locking his doors and windows and admitted only those customers he knew and trusted. "Some night, I'll be robbed of everything, but they'll have a tough job of getting in," he joked to customers, who hardly found this hilarious. Some complained of being inconvenienced; others wondered if Fink was perhaps teetering on the edge of paranoia.

As it turned out, Fink wasn't cautious enough.

## Breaking In

It's Saturday, March 9, 1929, a blustery day in the city of New York—temperatures drop as low as fifteen degrees. Fink's friend Ralph Sacks of Brooklyn stops by the laundry at about 1:00 p.m. He notices nothing unusual. That evening, Max Sternberg, the used-furniture salesman from across the street, also drops by the shop to say hi to Fink. Two customers show up briefly while Sternberg is there: Mary Merry and James Portest, frequent visitors who often bought used clothing from Fink.

By the time Sternberg leaves, it's 9:45 p.m., give or take.

Forty-five minutes later, Locklin Smith, an elderly lady who lives in an apartment building directly behind the laundry, is getting ready for bed. Smith's apartment is separated from the laundry by a securely nailed door that is never used.

She hears a commotion coming from the laundry. *Sounds like a scuffle*, she thinks. *Maybe some people arguing.* Then, more loud noises, like someone being struck on the head. Then, moaning. "Ike," someone says—maybe.

Locklin Smith—described in newspaper reports at the time as an "aged Negro"—is a brave woman. Instead of grabbing a pillow and placing it over her ears to drown out the noise, or willing herself into believing that whatever she thought she'd heard was merely a figment of her imagination, she yanks herself out of bed, huffs and puffs her way outside, and attempts to gain entry to the laundry.

Except the door is locked.

What to do? She stops a passerby on the street, whose name is lost to history, though we at least know he is a responsible citizen, because he consents to notify the police. At 10:42 p.m., he encounters Patrolman Albert Katterborn at the intersection of 132nd Street and Fifth Avenue and alerts him to the disturbance at Fink's shop.

Katterborn follows the Good Samaritan back to the laundry. He raps on the front door. No answer. He pushes his substantial frame against it. Nothing. Not even a budge. Obviously locked. The windows? Also locked. Not a bad idea in these parts. Katterborn tries taking a peek through the window, but this is New York in March; it's *maybe* twenty degrees, and the glass is frosted over. Katterborn can't see a damn thing except that the lights are on. Time to chat up Locklin Smith.

By the time he returns to the laundry, a crowd has gathered outside, including Officer Paul Lee, there to lend a hand. Glancing up, they spot a narrow transom window over the door, about seven feet above ground level. Any chance one of them can fit through it? Absolutely not. Way too small for either of them—or any normal-size adult, for that matter. Maybe they can find a kid to do it?

Meet Roseman Hull, a seventeen-year-old student whom police records will later describe as "small." Hull volunteers to crawl through the transom provided he can reach it, which he does by standing on Katterborn's shoulders. At first, the transom won't budge, but Hull perseveres, eventually forcing his way inside. He walks over to the front door and releases the seven-inch bolt, allowing Katterborn and Lee to enter.

Pretty cozy, this place: two rooms, front and back, about ten feet wide and thirty feet deep. In the front room, nothing strikes the coppers as out of place. In the back room, something does, *very*: Lying face down on the floor, arms outstretched, feet facing the front, is Isidore Fink. The officers noticed two bullet holes in the left side of the chest and one in the left wrist, where the bullet has passed through his thumb. Next to his body is an unclaimed bundle of laundry. Fink is unresponsive. He's not breathing. There's no pulse. Katterborn summons an ambulance; Fink is rushed to Harlem Hospital and pronounced dead.

### "THE PERFECT CRIME"?

The New York City coroner found that the gunshots to Fink's chest had caused irreparable damage to his heart, abdomen, liver, and gallbladder. He died instantly, or almost instantly. The killer had used .32-caliber steel-jacketed bullets. Fink's left hand had severe powder burns, indicating the shot had been fired at close range, possibly during a struggle for the weapon.

Meanwhile, back at the laundry, homicide cops had arrived and begun their investigation, now under the direction of Detective William Clark. A search for fingerprints turned up empty except for Fink's. They did find a hot iron on a lighted gas stove, suggesting Fink had been ironing when interrupted by his assassin. A bracket, broken off from the transom, was lying by one of Fink's feet. All the doors and windows had been locked from the inside, so how did the murderer escape? Fink died with money in his pockets and cash in the open register. If robbery wasn't the motive, what was?

Here's what they didn't find: the murder weapon. They searched inside and out; not a trace of it was revealed. They tore the place upside down looking for some sort of secret gun-wielding contraption that might have somehow automatically retreated into hiding after discharging the fatal shot, but again, nothing.

Could Fink have committed suicide? But again, where was the weapon? And why would Fink have shot himself in the wrist before firing the fatal shots to the chest? The coroner dismissed the hypothesis emphatically. "The man has been murdered," he said. "The position of the body and location of the wounds indicate, beyond doubt, that Fink could not have shot himself."

But who would want to murder a thirty-seven-year-old hardworking laundryman from Poland (or Russia)?

At the time of his death, Fink had lived for six months with a shoemaker named Max Schwartz in a large apartment building at 52 East 133rd Street in Harlem. He was single, and while his brother, Morris, lived not far away in the Bronx, the two were estranged. Every person interviewed told police that to the best of their knowledge, Frank didn't have a single enemy—nor many friends, for that matter. Schwartz contributed little; he told police Fink never talked about his personal life, though he did say his roommate had no female friends. (Early reports that Locklin Smith had spotted two "well-dressed" women near the laundry during her abortive investigation into the source of the noises she had heard were dismissed by police.)

After a two-year investigation, the best the NYPD could come up with was this: absolutely no one. On August 31, 1931, NYPD Commissioner Edward P. Mulrooney, appearing on WOR radio's *Man in the Front Row*, declared Fink's shooting an "insoluble mystery."

Newspapers of the time dubbed Fink's murder a "perfect crime." On March 11, 1929, the *Pittsburgh Press* labeled a United Press story "Perfect Plot: New York Police Can't Solve Riddle of Murder of Laundryman." That same day, the *Long Beach* (California) *Sun* headlined the same story "N.Y. Detectives Are Baffled by 'Perfect Crime.'" Similar headlines appeared in newspapers across the country.

But was Fink's murder *really* a perfect crime?

# N. Y. DETECTIVES ARE BAFFLED BY 'PERFECT CRIME'

Long Beach Fink
PHOTO COURTESY OF THE *LONG BEACH SUN*

## THEORIES

Police had plenty of theories to work with, some more plausible than others.

On March 10, the *New York Times* carried the story of Fink's death under the headline "Harlem Man Is Found Shot Dead by Assailant Who Entered Through Transom." This theory was predicated largely on the fact that police had found the bracket broken off from the transom on the floor of the laundry. But they eventually rejected this solution, perhaps because it still didn't explain how the killer had escaped; remember, the transom was seven feet above the ground, and nothing in the cops' investigation suggested that he had an accomplice who had boosted him up so that he could reach the transom either outside or inside the laundry. And even if he had, how then did the accomplice get out?

Could the killer have been someone Frank recognized and let in? Perhaps the killer fired the deadly shots, then escaped through the transom? Again unlikely, for the reasons stated above. Besides, who in their right mind would risk calling attention to himself at 10:30 p.m. on a Saturday by climbing through the transom and leaping seven feet to the ground when he could just as easily have walked out the front door?

But what if the killer hadn't escaped through the transom, but rather hid in the laundry and eluded police by exiting undetected amid all the hubbub as authorities conducted their investigation inside and civilians gathered outside? The problem with this theory was that police had turned the place upside down looking for some kind of remote-control contraption that Fink might have used to fire the gun himself. (In "The Bird House," an Isidore Fink–inspired short story by William March, the killer, trapped inside the apartment after the shooting, flattens himself against the wall by the door; once the door is opened, he slips into the entryway and is pushed forward by the gathering crowd outside, finally disappearing into the horde of people.) In 1997, the *Detroit Jewish News* asked readers to write in with their own solutions to the Fink murder. The *News* selected two winning essays, one by Esther Littman and the residents of the Fountain of Franklin senior living center, in which the two well-dressed women supposedly spotted by Locklin Smith were actually two well-dressed men in disguise who gunned down Fink in retribution for some unspecified treason he had committed against them; and the other by Lucille Miller, who fingered the killer as an imaginary Isaac "Ike" Rabinowich, whose sister Gittle had been impregnated by Fink back in Odessa but killed herself after losing the baby.

Could the killer, unable to gain entry to the laundry, have stood on something—or someone—outside the door and fired the shots through the open transom window, then slammed the transom shut before leaving? The answer was no, because the scorch marks on Fink's hand indicated a close-range shooting.

Could the police themselves have been involved in Fink's death and a cover-up, tampering with evidence and falsifying their report? No evidence ever suggested it.

This leaves us then with the most likely theory: What if Fink knew the killer, so opened the door to let them in? Perhaps an argument ensued as the killer waited in the hallway outside the door. Fink could have been shot from the hallway, then stumbled back inside the laundry and bolted the door behind him to ensure the killer couldn't follow him inside. Or perhaps Fink had allowed the killer to enter, the shooting occurred inside the laundry, and the killer jack-rabbited immediately after firing the shot? Back in 1929, this theory was adamantly dismissed by the coroner, who insisted that the wounds Fink suffered would have killed him almost instantaneously, making it impossible for Fink to retreat inside the laundry, bolt the door behind him, and walk through the front room before collapsing in the back. But more recently, medical experts like Emily Entzi Narciso, a physician's assistant in California who worked in emergency medicine, was quoted in a paid Facebook Watch piece that ran in the *New York Times*: "You could run 25 feet if shot in the chest, depending on where the bullet hit. I've seen people drive themselves to the emergency department after being shot and then simply run through the front door." Emergency room doctors in New York City subsequently confirmed Narciso's analysis.

In 2023, HubPage's C. C. Brooks discovered an article from the British *Police Journal* in which an eminent pathologist by the name of Sir Sydney Smith recounted the unusual case of a Scottish businessman who left his room in an Edinburgh hotel one winter evening and didn't return until 7:30 a.m. the following day. Spotted by the maid, the man appeared perfectly ordinary—except for his bloodstained face. "Think I'll go up and have a wash," he told the maid, calmly hanging up his coat and stashing his umbrella on the rack. Which he did, upstairs in the bathroom, where he collapsed; three hours later, he was pronounced dead at a hospital, without being able to tell authorities anything about the events of the previous night. The man had been shot in the chin at close range with a .45-caliber gun; the bullet wound its way up into the brain, causing massive damage. Smith was convinced that the shooting—eventually determined to be by the man's own hand—had occurred several hours before he died. "Smith was flabbergasted," Brooks wrote. "The man had blown away a sizable chunk of his own brain, and yet lived and walked for several hours, even talking coherently, before finally losing consciousness." Smith wrote that any medical person, on seeing such a massive injury, would have automatically assumed a near-instantaneous death. He called it "a striking example of what can be done after a severe injury to the brain."

This certainly would appear to contradict the New York coroner's conclusion that given the nature of his injuries, Fink couldn't possibly have bolted the door himself and stayed alive until reaching the back room of the laundry. As true crime writer Keven McQueen told Facebook Watch, "Only two people could possibly have slid the door's bolt, Fink or his killer. And since it was impossible for the killer to have done it [since he apparently had no way of escaping once the door was bolted], it must have been Fink."

Those unswayed by this theory argue that the police report makes no mention of finding blood tracks in the hallway or anywhere between the front door and the rear room, where Fink eventually collapsed. Could Fink's clothing have absorbed all the blood?

Assuming this theory is true, we're still left with two stubborn mysteries: Who killed Fink, and why?

If in fact Fink had opened the door for the killer, the implication is that it was someone he knew and trusted, since he was particular about whom he allowed in. Max Sternberg, the used-furniture salesman from across the street, claimed to have visited Fink briefly at about 9:45 p.m. on the night of the murder but left when he saw his friend engaged in a discussion with Mary Merry and James Portest, who were looking to buy secondhand underwear from Frink (gross, but true, maybe: In those days laundries did sell unclaimed clothing). Sternberg claimed the couple were Black, which isn't insignificant: "The linking of Black people with criminality was very much part of society at the time," Kevin McGruder, an associate professor of history at Antioch College in Ohio, told Facebook Watch. "The idea was that wherever Black people go, they bring crime. That fueled a resistance movement in Harlem." McGruder wasn't buying Sternberg's claim either that the couple were on the prowl for secondhand underwear: "People asking for unclaimed underwear doesn't seem likely to me. If they're buying anything used, underwear is probably not it. Not even then." Police never tracked down the couple, though it's unclear how earnestly they tried. Had Sternberg and Fink argued over something? Did Sternberg invent his story to deflect suspicion from himself? But why even volunteer to police that he had dropped by the laundry that night so close to the time of death? Police didn't even consider Sternberg a suspect.

As for motive, nobody seemed to have a clue.

Charles Fort, author of *The Book of the Damned*, a landmark work in the exploration of paranormal phenomena, wondered if Fink was haunted by a "specific fear, of somebody whom he had harmed, and not a general fear of the hold-ups that, at the time, were so prevalent in New York City"—but Fort was just speculating, without any evidence to back it up. Ben Hecht's 1931 short story "The Mystery of the Fabulous Laundryman," a thinly veiled and thickly embellished account of Fink's murder, fueled rumors that perhaps Fink had led a double life. In the story by Hecht, who is best known as the coauthor of the journalism-themed comedy *The Front Page*, the murdered laundryman is really the czar of Russia, hiding out from assassins. While no one ever suspected Fink of being exiled Russian royalty, there was the matter of those two "well-dressed" women Locklin Smith reportedly saw on the night of the murder, though police never gave it much credence.

The murder of Isidore Fink has never been solved, and the case remains open. The final police report was filed on August 15, 1930, as detectives continued to interview Fink's associates.

Fink is buried at the Mount Richmond Cemetery on Staten Island.

RIP, Isidore Fink. Gone but certainly not forgotten.

## 9

# Who Ordered the Cement Shoes?

## *New York City*

Abraham "Bo" Weinberg was having a busy year in 1935 before he suddenly vanished without a trace early that September. Bo was a career thug, having grown up on the mean streets of the Bronx in the early years of the twentieth century. By 1935 he was a top lieutenant for Dutch Schultz, one of the most dangerous and infamous gangsters of the era. Schultz had been a fugitive from the law for nearly two years when he finally turned himself in the fall of the previous year to face trial for income tax invasion. With his boss on the run in upstate New York, it fell upon Bo and others of the Dutchman's inner circle to keep operations running smoothly.

And while business was still good, it wasn't roaring like in the glory days of Prohibition. The repeal of the Volstead Act in 1933 had basically put an end to the bootlegging career of the "Beer Baron of the Bronx"—a moniker Schultz had earned during his violent and bloody rise to kingpin that effectively controlled the flow of liquor throughout his not inconsiderable territory in New York City. With beer legal again, the Schultz gang was forced to diversify, branching out into protection racketeering, illegal lotteries, and horse racing, and even dabbling in training heavyweight boxers.

The gang was still raking in the cash, but business was more complicated than in the old days. There was fierce competition from entrenched interests, and new rivals were always emerging in their chosen lines of business—not to mention that the barriers to entry into these new markets often resulted in dead bodies. It was during these turbulent times, with Schultz forced into hiding because of pressure from the likes of crusading Special Prosecutor Thomas Dewey and

FBI Director J. Edgar Hoover, who had recently labeled Schultz Public Enemy Number One, that Bo was thrust into more of a decision-making role, instead of being the one taking orders.

In April 1935, Schultz was finally put on trial in Syracuse for tax evasion, resulting in a hung jury after two days of deliberations. A subsequent trial took place a few months later in the tiny village of Malone, New York, just fifteen miles south of the Canadian border. Bo and several of his associates were summoned from the Big Apple to appear as a witness at both trials. In the past, Bo had been, to put it mildly, somewhat hesitant to testify in court, adhering to the organized crime ethos of revealing nothing to the law—not even the identity of a sworn enemy who had taken a shot at you.

When he did testify, Bo pleaded the Fifth Amendment, saying that any of his testimony might incriminate him; his associates also either pleaded the Fifth or developed faulty memories. Despite the gangsters' unwillingness to confirm any of the particulars, the prosecution presented a seemingly rock-solid case against Schultz, clearly illustrating the large sums of money his organization had taken in without paying any federal taxes. Despite this preponderance of evidence against him, Schultz defied the odds, receiving a verdict of not guilty on August 2.

After thwarting the latest swipe from the hand of justice, Schultz declined to return to NYC and instead set up operations in New Jersey; NYC Mayor Fiorello La Guardia, newly elected on a reform platform, had publicly stated that despite the outcome of the two trials, Schultz wasn't welcome back home. And so his loyal lieutenant, Bo Weinberg, was sent back to mind the store.

A month or so later, people started noticing that Bo hadn't been hanging around his usual haunts. A September 28 interview in the *Daily News* with Alice Wallace revealed that she was Bo's wife, with the pair having tied the knot in March of that year; secret marriages revealed after the death of a gangster were relatively commonplace in that era. Alice claimed she had not seen Bo since September 9, when she was with him at a Midtown hotel, and had no idea as to his current whereabouts. Bo Weinberg was never seen again publicly, and his body has never been found, although most theories about what happened assign the Hudson or East River as his final resting place.

# Bo

Abraham "Bo" Weinberg (he was nicknamed Bo because of his bowed legs, which caused an unusual gait) was born to Samuel and Gussie Weinberg in Manhattan on January 7, 1900. He grew up to become an intimidating figure:

of medium height but squat and muscular, described uncharitably as both resembling and speaking like an underworld gorilla. The one word used most often to describe the personality of the lifelong hood was "sullen."

Bo's parents were Austrian Jewish immigrants who didn't speak English when they came to America a few years before he was born. His father worked as a laundryman and sometimes tailor while his mother tended to the household of seven active children; Bo was the third oldest, although his older brother Zelig died as a toddler, after having survived the voyage across the Atlantic.

Big Bo Weinberg

*DAILY NEWS*

Samuel passed away in 1911 at the age of forty-four due to heart failure, just around the time when young Bo started hanging out on the streets and meeting the "wrong sorts" who would so heavily influence his path in life. The Weinbergs moved across the bridge, from southern Manhattan, into downtown Brooklyn, a fertile breeding ground for many of the toughs who would dominate the streets over the following decades. Young Bo worked as an errand boy and later drove a taxicab, but was soon tempted into more rewarding, if less savory, pursuits.

In July 1920, while still ostensibly working as a taxi driver, Bo employed his skills as the getaway driver for a botched bank robbery. Bo sat idling outside the Corona branch of the Bank of Manhattan around lunchtime while his cohorts were inside demanding money from the surprised clerk. Remarkably, the clerk somehow turned the tables on them, bombarding the robbers with inkpads, until they eventually fled empty-handed. The following night, Bo was recognized by a police officer who had witnessed the would-be robbers streaking from the bank, resulting in a stint at the Queens jail at Long Island City.

Rather than treat this incident as a youthful indiscretion and life lesson, Bo was arrested less than a year later on a robbery-and-assault charge that led to a longer sentence, served in Sing Sing prison, thirty miles north of Manhattan in the town of Ossining. Bo emerged from Sing Sing older and hardened, into the nascent boom days of organized crime, triggered by the start of Prohibition. The recently passed Volstead Act prohibited the sale and consumption of alcohol in the United States, but the nation's demand for booze would not be legislated away so easily. Similarly, the passage of the Volstead Act didn't anticipate the swell in the criminal ranks that this persistent demand would create. This was a world ripe for the picking for tough, opportunistic, and hungry men like Bo Weinberg—men who would do whatever it took to make a buck as long as they thought they could get away with it.

In the early 1920s, Bo was working as a beer runner for "the original Bronx Beer Baron," Harry Drucker, and had become one of his top men. Around this time, he first encountered Arthur Flegenheimer, a new recruit to the Drucker gang, recently released from prison himself. Flegenheimer, soon to earn his more familiar moniker of Dutch Schultz—an homage to a notorious nineteenth-century Bronx gang leader—approached Bo and another Drucker lieutenant, Little Augie, one day with a proposal: The ambitious Flegenheimer, whom Drucker had been using as muscle, thought that the three of them could take out their boss and split his criminal empire three ways. Bo and Little Augie considered the proposal, and before too long Drucker's lifeless body was found riddled with bullets. The trio were questioned in the aftermath, but of course they knew nothing. Soon after, Dutch Schultz emerged as the new Beer Baron of the Bronx, continuing to expand his territory and influence throughout the Roaring Twenties, and during most of the Dutchman's infamous criminal escapades, Bo was at his side, usually in a prominent, and often ruthlessly violent, role.

## A LIFE OF CRIME

Dutch Schultz's rise to the top of the criminal underworld kept Bo very busy. Bo was truly his right-hand man, attending all the big meetings and participating in key decision-making, but he was also the top heavy in the gang, whom you went to if you had a problem that needed solving: robbery, intimidation, assault, and murder. There is no doubt that Bo did his share of these crimes and more, although it must be remembered that the details of these exploits are somewhat undermined because of the kinds of witnesses who were telling the stories. Many of the killings Bo was said to have participated in were based on the word of Dixie Davis, Schultz's lawyer, who was eventually put on trial himself for his role in the Dutchman's criminal empire. Reporter Paul Sann, in his 1971 account of Dutch's life and death titled *Kill the Dutchman!*, observed that Davis had a penchant for weaving the facts to suit his needs: "In his more talkative years, the counselor developed a habit of crediting the lovable Bo with almost any murder that you might ask about or even if you didn't."

Perhaps the most infamous murder that Bo was purported to be involved with was that of Arnold Rothstein, the legendary kingpin of the criminal underworld; Rothstein put the "organized" in organized crime, adapting his empire to a businesslike model that favored collaboration over violence when possible. Rothstein, aka "The Brain" and "The Bigman," was instrumental in mentoring the careers of notorious gangsters such as Lucky Luciano, Bugsy Siegel, Meyer Lansky, and even Schultz himself.

Rothstein also had a severe gambling addiction—his mathematical prowess had won him thousands of dollars over the years as he found ways to beat the system. However, that addiction may have caught up with him on November 4, 1928, when The Brain was shot at a hotel in Manhattan, dying from his wounds two days later. Gangland lore held that Rothstein had lost a fortune in a recent poker game but claimed the game was rigged and refused to pay. George McManus, one of the players whom Rothstein accused of being in on the fix, allegedly was the man who pulled the trigger. McManus was tried but acquitted due to a lack of evidence; even Rothstein, as he lay dying in the hospital, refused to identify his attacker to police, telling detectives, "Me mudder did it."

In *Kill the Dutchman!* Sann asserts that the Rothstein slaying was actually an exchange in a larger gangland war between Schultz and Jack "Legs" Diamond, a rival gangster and associate of Rothstein who was responsible for the death of Schultz's partner Joey Noy. As part of the payback for Noy, McManus did the deed, with Bo once again driving the getaway car. Bo was also reportedly part of the team that ended the war with Diamond in December 1931; after being driven out of NYC, Diamond had been on the run in upstate New York for several months when he was finally tracked down at a hotel in Albany. Diamond, who had survived being shot multiple times during the previous few years, had drunkenly passed out in his hotel room in the early hours of the morning. Around 5:30 a.m., a pair of gunmen—one of whom was allegedly Bo—burst into the room and pounced on the defenseless Diamond. One man held Legs down while the other executed him, firing three shots into the back of the head, finally taking out organized crime's version of Rasputin.

The Schultz gang's most bloody conflict grew out of internal strife when Joey Noy, the Dutchman's original partner, was murdered in a November 1928 hit, leaving a perceived leadership gap in the organization. Vincent "Mad Dog" Coll was an Irish immigrant who had joined up with Schultz's crew in the late 1920s as a hired gun guarding beer delivery trucks. He was another troubled kid who had consistently run afoul of the law, leading to twenty-three arrests by the age of twenty-three. Coll flourished in the gang, becoming an assassin who specialized in eliminating owners of rival speakeasies who had been less than open to Dutch's propositions to exclusively sell his brand of liquor.

As time went on, the ambitious, if somewhat unstable, Coll entreated Dutch to accept him as a partner. When Noy, Dutch's longtime pal and the only person he ever considered a true equal in his criminal enterprises, was assassinated by rival gang members, Coll seized on the opportunity; he offered to take Noy's place at Dutch's side. Schultz wasn't interested in a new partner and declined Coll's proposition, leaving both men simmering with resentment.

Coll responded to the snub by initiating his own rogue operations, without first obtaining Schultz's blessing. In a novel start to his crime spree, he robbed a dairy in the Bronx, netting around $18,000; soon after, a full-blown gangland war that would last nearly two years erupted between the two factions. As with much of the history of gangster killings, it can be hard to get reliable reports because of extremely reluctant witnesses, but the war ended up costing the lives of an estimated twenty soldiers from both sides, including Coll's brother Peter.

In one notable exchange, Coll and his men were attempting to take out a Schultz bootlegger standing guard outside a nightclub. The bootlegger cottoned on and quickly dove for cover before the ambush took hold; unfortunately, four schoolchildren ended up being shot by Coll and his men, including five-year-old Michael Vengalli, who would tragically die of his injuries a few days after the botched shooting. Soon after, NYC's Mayor Jimmy Walker was raging against "Mad Dog" Coll in the press—not the most flattering of nicknames, but Coll likely preferred it to another that had emerged: "Baby Killer."

By early 1932, Schultz had gained the upper hand in his long, chaotic war with Coll; the Mad Dog had barely survived multiple attempts on his life, and both Schultz and another gangster rival, Owney Madden, had each put $50,000 bounties on Coll's head. As a result of the intense heat, Coll had been on the run for months when he finally ran out of luck on February 8, 1932. He was staying at the Cornish Arms Hotel with his wife, Lottie, and had gone out to a nearby chemist to take an arranged call from Madden. As Madden stalled him on the phone, a limousine driven by Bo Weinberg pulled up to the phone booth. Two men jumped out and earned their $50,000, tommy-gunning Coll to smithereens before escaping in the vehicle that Bo drove hastily away from the crime scene.

While Bo's exact roles in the murders detailed above are obscured by the veil of silence that unified nearly all members of the criminal underworld, it seems inarguable that he was responsible for a good deal of violence over his lifetime;

more often than not, the lives of such men end one way—badly.

## THE END OF AN ERA

By 1935, the reign of Dutch Schultz was coming to an end, and with hindsight the writing had clearly been on the wall for some time. The repeal of the Volstead Act in December 1933 not only ended the nationwide ban on alcohol, it also had a seismic impact on the criminal underworld. Beer running had been Schultz's primary trade, and he now needed to diversify. The Dutchman had gotten ahead of some of these coming changes, forcibly inserting himself into the profitable Harlem policy racket, aka "playing the numbers," that had been a tradition in the community for years.

NEWSPAPERS.COM

The racket was essentially an illegal lottery that used supposedly random public numbers, such as the day's final stock exchange digits or the total amount of money bet on a particular horse race, to determine the winner. Numbers had been operating, largely nonviolently, in Harlem for generations, until Schultz identified the racket as a potential lucrative income stream and aggressively inserted himself into the market. Intimidation, threats, and, when "necessary," violence followed, until Schultz eventually took effective control of the whole system.

Thanks to the numbers game, as well as other endeavors, such as restaurant protection rackets and the extortion of organized workers, Schultz was still getting by just fine, but moving into new enterprises with established competition took its toll over time on his organization. And often in the criminal underworld, weakness is enough to expose even the most powerful bosses.

The 1930s also brought a wave of reform driven at the national level by the administration of President Franklin Delano Roosevelt. The press, too, played a major role in exposing widespread institutional corruption, including ties between criminals and politicians, such as those between Dutch Schultz and Tammany Hall boss Jimmy Hines; Hines was sent to prison in 1938 by then Manhattan District Attorney Thomas E. Dewey. Dewey, a straight-shooting former federal prosecutor on a crusade against organized crime, eventually rose to the level of Democratic nominee for president in 1948—he is the Dewey of the infamously hasty "Dewey Defeats Truman" headline. Dewey ultimately proved to be a nemesis for Dutch Schultz.

Schultz was getting hit with more subpoenas, and the cops weren't always looking the other way, as once had been routine. With the spotlight on, Schultz left NYC, moving around upstate New York as a fugitive from justice. In November 1934 he finally decided to turn himself in on charges of tax evasion— the same crime that had Chicago boss Al Capone serving an eleven-year sentence in federal prison. Bo was among those summoned to testify in Syracuse in April 1935. Perhaps not unexpectedly, Bo, surly from being pulled away from his business in the city, had an extremely faulty memory when called to the stand. Schultz's trial in Syracuse ended with a hung jury, and a new trial was scheduled in Malone for later that summer,

Once again a disgruntled Bo was subpoenaed, and he reluctantly traveled upstate to testify. In the preliminary stages of the trial, federal judge Frederick H. Bryant sequestered Bo and three of his colleagues, having them stay in jail for the duration of the trial. The locals sniggered as the burly Bo and his big-city confederates were dragged off to the sweltering cells of the county jail, having previously been staying at the best hotel suites in town. Bo simmered as he was escorted from the courtroom by the marshal, "resplendent in a smoke gray summer suit and blue polo shirt."

And yet despite the stay in prison, Bo remained defiant when called to the stand, reading a lengthy prepared statement asserting that by answering any questions about Schultz's income he could potentially violate his own constitutional rights. Under direct questioning, he did admit to knowing Schultz, whom he had met fourteen years earlier. But as for the Dutchman's reign as the Bronx Beer Baron or any other illegal activities, Bo didn't have a clue as to what they were talking about. Other Schultz associates called as witnesses were equally uncooperative. Still, despite the witnesses' refusal to discuss the Schultz empire, the pile of hard evidence that Dewey's team had presented to the jury should have rendered the decision an easy one. And yet Schultz was deemed not guilty and free to go, leaving the judge to fume at the decision, citing the incontrovertible facts proving Schultz had failed to pay taxes on income he had taken in.

Apparently, the Dutchman's decision to move to the tiny town of Malone a month before the trial—buying round after round night after night for the locals (and future jury members), becoming chummy with both the mayor and sheriff, even hiring a local lawyer to be his mouthpiece at the trial—might have had some effect on the jury's deliberations. Schultz had won the round, but Dewey was relentless, and another trial loomed.

After the Malone trial ended, Bo returned to NYC to resume effective control of Schultz's operations. A month or so later, in late September, newspapers started to report that Bo hadn't been seen around town at his usual haunts lately; this was unexpected, as his daily routine would take him around to nightclubs, restaurants, and other public settings to make sure business was running smoothly. Once word of Bo's disappearance got out, everyone seemed to have a different theory about what had happened to him; he was definitely dead, or perhaps he was alive but in hiding from either the law or rival gangsters. Even those who agreed he was dead disagreed on the specifics: He might have been buried in a grave of quicklime, or had he been, perhaps, dissolved in a strong chemical solution?

Rumors abounded regarding what Bo's disappearance meant; members of the Schultz gang were cagey when questioned. Some speculated that he was taken out as part of a gang war, which likely portended an escalation in violence from both sides. Word had it that Schultz's revenge squads were already out looking for Bo's killer, with Dutch and his surviving inner circle "gripped with impotent fury." The police were sure that Bo's slaying was part of a gangland war involving the rival Amberg family, who had splintered off from Schultz some time earlier. Other known associates claimed Bo was just out of town, either lying low or taking care of business, depending on whom you asked. Maybe he was in California? No, he's hiding out in Colorado, but he'll be back any day now.

One specific story purported that Bo had overheard someone disparaging Little Marty Krompier, another Schultz lieutenant; Bo took offense, and the ensuing scuffle resulted in Bo being riddled with bullets.

Over time, the legend of Bo's fate evolved from a simple gangland shooting to a more dramatic demise, a scenario still talked about as a gangster cliché today: Bo was sleeping with the fishes in the East Hudson River, dumped in the water with the lower half of his body encased in fast-acting cement to ensure he didn't easily leave the seabed.

The day following the initial reports about Bo being missing surfaced, Dutch Schultz was arrested in Perth Amboy, New Jersey, after a federal judge in Newark issued a bench warrant; although he had twice been acquitted, additional charges

Dutch Schultz
*DAILY NEWS*

loomed. The local police tried to tie Schultz to a recent robbery of a train ticket agency but were unable to produce enough evidence to hold him. G-men wanted the locals to hold Schultz, but by the time they arrived in Perth Amboy, he had been released due to the lack of evidence. If the Dutchman knew what was just around the corner, he might have chosen to surrender there and then. Rather, Schultz appeared to relocate his home base to Newark, creeping closer back to NYC, where, in the wake of Bo's mysterious disappearance, operations were now being seen to by Dutch's lawyer, Dixie Davis.

On the evening of October 23, 1935, Schultz was holding court at the Palace Chop House and Tavern on East Park Street in Newark. He had settled into a routine of spending most of his business hours there over the past three weeks or so. That night Schultz had been in the restaurant for several hours, attending to a variety of affairs and speaking with many visitors, including Frances Flegenheimer, his twenty-four-year-old bride, who had spent about an hour with Dutch earlier in the afternoon, before their visit was abruptly curtailed by the arrival of a bondsman who needed to discuss Schultz's payments. Business proceeded over the course of the evening until a little after 10 p.m., when Schultz excused himself to use the lavatory located in the back corner of the restaurant.

Around 10:15 p.m., a stocky, muscular man with dark curly hair calmly entered the restaurant and approached Jack Friedman, the forty-four-year-old barman, who up to that point had been bored by the slow business and was now cleaning up around the bar. The interloper had his topcoat pulled up high to obscure the details of his face as he instructed the bartender, "Don't move. Lay down." Friedman later recalled, "I saw him place his hand on his left shoulder and whip out a gun from a holster. I didn't wait any longer. I dropped to the floor and lay behind the bar."

As Friedman quickly found a good hiding place, the man who had warned him, later described to be in his mid-thirties, continued toward the back of the restaurant and was joined by a colleague, who was taller and older than the first man. The pair moved like professionals, silently heading to the back, where they expected to find the Dutchman waiting. They greeted his compatriots with guns blazing; the tall man fired round after round from a .38-caliber pistol while his burly pal supported him with blasts from the sawed-off shotgun he had hidden under his coat.

All three of Schultz's men on the scene eventually died from the gunshots fired by the pair of assassins. Lulu Rosenkrantz was one of Dutch's top bodyguards; Abe Landau, older and more experienced, was also hired muscle; and the third victim, Otto "Abbadabba" Berman, was valued by Schultz more for his mathematical intellect—the odd, pudgy little man was behind successful schemes that had optimized Schultz's profits in the policy rackets. Despite the devastation unleashed by the two gunmen, their main quarry was nowhere to be seen. However, it didn't take long to locate the out-of-the-way restroom in the back corner, where a surprised and defenseless Schultz wound up taking a bullet in the abdomen that tore through his large intestine, gallbladder, and liver.

Schultz would die the next day in a Newark hospital, babbling away in a nearly psychedelic stream of consciousness, fueled by heavy medication and the pain from his gunshot wounds. His nonsensical rant has mystified enthusiasts ever since—perhaps there was a clue as to where the Dutchman's rumored secret fortune, never found, was located. Or perhaps Bo Weinberg's fate was hidden in one of Schultz's cryptic deathbed mutterings, which included such insights as this response to a question about who had shot him: "Please put me up on my feet at once. Thank you, Sam, you are a boiled man; I do it because you asked me to. Did you hear me? I would hear it, the Circuit Court would hear it, and the Supreme Court might hear it. Come on, pull me up, sir. All right. Cam Davis. Oh, please reply. N.R.A. If that ain't the payoff. Please crack down on the Chinaman's friends and Hitler's commander. . . . Mother is the best bet and don't let Satan draw you too fast."

Over time it would emerge that Schultz likely met his end because of tensions with a powerful confederation of rival crime lords, unofficially referred to as the National Crime Syndicate, or sometimes merely the Syndicate. The Syndicate consisted of notorious criminal luminaries such as Lucky Luciano, Arnold Rothstein, and Bugsy Siegel. Schultz was associated with them, but following the turbulence his business had undergone in the wake of the repeal of Prohibition, coupled with Thomas Dewey's relentless drive to bring him to justice, he was excluded as one of its senior members.

As the heat from Dewey was mounting, Schultz had come up with his own strategy to deal with the problem—one that called for Dewey to be gunned down in a hail of bullets. He went before the Syndicate to seek approval. The committee weighed the pros and cons of such an audacious move and decided that taking out the special prosecutor would only fuel the heat they were feeling from crusaders like Eliot Ness and J. Edgar Hoover. Incensed, Schultz vowed to take care of Dewey himself; this did not sit well with senior members of the Syndicate, and soon plans were being hatched to send experienced members of Murder Inc., the branch of the Syndicate that handled assassinations, to take care of the Schultz problem at the Palace Chop House in Newark.

## Veil of Silence

The details of the Shultz hit would come out over the following years as Dewey and other investigators were able to gradually turn insiders with offers of plea deals; such stool pigeons were rare and valuable because of the unspoken criminal code that nobody talked to the cops. This surely was why Dutch Schultz refused to give the police any information on who had shot him even as he lay dying in the hospital. Those few informants who did give evidence against their former compatriots did so for a reason, usually to escape their own punishment. In that regard, the historical record of organized crime is tainted by an abundance of unreliable narrators—this should be considered when examining the murders of both Dutch and Bo Weinberg.

And while the circumstances behind Dutch's murder do seem to have been more or less resolved, the answer to what happened to Bo Weinberg remains much more shrouded in whispers and gangland lore. Indeed, since his body went undiscovered, there was never any official investigation into his death. However, shortly after Dutch was gunned down, a little more than a month after Bo had gone missing, gossip about what had happened to Bo started to veer off in a new direction.

At first, it was reported that it was actually Bo who had been behind Dutch's execution—he had been in hiding for the past several weeks and finally emerged looking to take over operations permanently, according to this new speculation. Rumors surfaced that Bo had been seen, very much alive, at Madison Square Garden for a heavyweight fight in November 1935, although when police investigated the story, they found no trace of him. The story of Bo being behind the Schultz hit evolved into a scenario where he and gangster lawyer Dixie Davis had schemed together to take out Schultz. It wasn't long, after having rubbed out Dutch, that Dixie then supposedly double-crossed Bo and had him executed in turn.

Less than twenty-four hours before Schultz and his men were taken out in Newark, Louis "Pretty" Amberg was axed to death and then set ablaze, leading reporters and lawmen to once again speculate that a gang war with the Ambergs had been the reason for the slayings of both Bo and Schultz. According to this account, Bo had approached two "money lenders" who were employed by the Ambergs back in August, inviting them to come work for the Schultz gang, the job offers laced with not-so-subtle threatening undertones. The men reported the incident back to the Ambergs, who responded by sending a delegation to not only decline Bo's request, but to assault and kidnap him. Bo was then taken and held in an unknown hangout on the east side of town until after the Shultz shooting. Bo was no longer seen as a potential asset, and his body was soon dumped with little ceremony somewhere across the Queensboro River.

The story that most would come to believe was that Bo had been dead since at least early September, long before Schultz was killed. In fact, now that Schultz was out of the picture, gossip from anonymous sources started to point the finger at the Dutchman himself as the one who had taken out his top man. These sources painted a picture of Dutch losing his grip in his final days, having been out of town on the lam and more focused on fending off Thomas Dewey than on his organization's day-to-day operations. Bo had been effectively running things for a while now; maybe he thought he should be running things permanently.

Reports had Bo covertly building up his own personal army of loyal soldiers and scheming with Schultz's rivals to make some sort of deal. In this scenario, Bo had seen the writing on the wall: Schultz had been on the run and out of touch for nearly two years, and it didn't seem likely he would be back for good any time soon. He had twice beaten charges in court, but Dewey was relentless, and it was only a matter of time before his boss went down for tax evasion, like Al Capone before him.

One source pointed to Little Marty Krompier as the Schultz man who was responsible for offing Bo—Krompier was the same man whose honor Bo had been defending when he was slain by members of the rival Amberg gang in another version of Bo's death, reported a month prior. Now, supposedly Krompier had discovered that Bo was skimming money off the top of payoffs and subsequently arranged for him to meet his end in a nameless hotel room.

Regardless of whether it was one of his men like Krompier or Schultz himself, over the decades, gangland lore and eventually popular culture seemed to have settled on the theory that it was the Dutchman himself who had taken out Bo because of his perceived betrayal. It was believed that a suspicious Schultz had Bo tailed until he was seen coming out of a meeting with Long East Zwilman, a mob boss from New Jersey, who was associated with Lucky Luciano. Bo was said to have basically offered control of Schultz's operations to the Syndicate. He had seen Schultz's influence diminish, and the relentless Dewey seemed destined to put Schultz behind bars sooner or later. Bo wanted to retain control of day-to-day operations and receive 15 percent of the take; Luciano had concerns about moving prematurely against Schultz but took Bo's offer to the other members of the Syndicate.

Further, gangland lore and popular culture have coalesced around the idea that Schultz was so enraged that he wanted Bo to not only die, but to suffer ignominiously. And so while either still alive or already dead, depending on the version, Bo was encased in a quick-drying soft cement mix. Once it hardened, Bo was dumped off the side of a boat in the East Hudson River, the whole incident serving as early inspiration for the expression, made famous in *The Godfather*, "he sleeps with the fishes."

And yet, this version of how Bo came to his end, while dramatic, even cinematic, is based largely on those gangland whispers and rumors discussed previously, exaggerated and distorted over the years. Lost in the mists of time were other rumors that came out in the wake of Bo's disappearance, pointing the finger at a different culprit: the Syndicate. Tensions were high between the Schultz gang and the Syndicate during this period, culminating a month later in the hit of Schultz at the Palace Chop House in Newark. Could the Syndicate have been sending Schultz a message by taking out his head of operations?

If Schultz had ignored this and other warnings to back off from his plan to assassinate Dewey, maybe the go-ahead was finally given to take him out. Additionally, the Syndicate would eventually absorb much of the Dutchman's empire after Schultz, Bo, and others in their gang went down, ending up either in jail or underground (or underwater). With Schultz out of the picture, it would have been easy, and convenient—the members of the Syndicate were starting to feel plenty of heat from Dewey themselves—to point the finger at the newly deceased Schultz for Bo's murder.

In all likelihood, the truth behind Bo Weinberg's disappearance will never be known. The passage of time and organized crime's self-imposed ban on disclosing inside business to the outside world casts a heavy shadow over the truth of events. If you squealed, you were dead to your old friends, sometimes quite literally; very few witnesses from that time went on the record. Those few who did, including Dixie Davis, who was left holding the bag after Dewey continued to dismantle Schultz's organization following his death, had selfish motives for ratting out their colleagues.

The murky history of organized crime in the early twentieth century at least casts some doubt on the widely accepted myth of Dutch providing the cement shoes for Bo. It was only after Schultz was taken out of the picture a month after Bo had disappeared that he began to emerge as the leading suspect—a narrative that would benefit any other potential suspect, such as the Syndicate or even the rival Amberg gang. It would be easy enough to start those whispers in order to help take the heat off the Syndicate for Bo's murder, when they too were finding themselves targeted by Dewey and others like him.

It seems unlikely the fate of Bo Weinberg will ever truly be known; the inherently unreliable nature of the few relevant witnesses who did speak on the record, coupled with the fact that there was never any official public investigation into his death, as his likely submerged corpse would have been needed to initiate proceedings, leaves the case shrouded in mystery. And so, it seems that the story cemented in E. L. Doctorow's popular novel, and the subsequent cinematic adaptation, *Billy Bathgate*, that Bo Weinberg sleeps with the fishes, will have to do.

# 10
# The Bomb Heard 'Round the World's Fair

## *Queens*

If only Superman had arrived a day later. On Wednesday, July 3, 1940, the New York World's Fair presented Superman Day, which featured a flurry of activities culminating in the crowning of one Superboy and one Supergirl by a panel of judges. Superman himself appeared (possibly Broadway's Ray Middleton), a "resplendent figure," as the *New York Times* phrased it, poised on a marble pedestal as he steered the parade of Boy Scouts, clowns, and Asian elephants along the fairgrounds. All in all, a huge success, even if one mom stormed off when her son played the game of thrones—and lost.

At around 5:00 p.m. the following day, a bomb planted in the British Pavilion detonated, tearing a crater five feet wide and four feet deep in the ground and splintering windows in the Polish Pavilion more than one hundred feet away. "Hats, strips of clothing, shoes and fragments of bodies were hurled through the air over a 50-foot radius," according to the *New York Daily News*. The blast stripped a nearby maple tree of its leaves and most of its bark, twisting and tearing the heavy wire fence enclosing the grounds. At first, many people thought the explosion was part of the Fourth of July celebration—fireworks had been going off all day—but within minutes, thousands of attendees had crowded around the site of the explosion as ambulances, police, and World's Fair guards rushed to the scene.

Detective Joseph Lynch, a member of the New York Police Department's bomb squad, died instantly. His partner, Detective Ferdinand Socha, lost both his feet; he struggled to stand up, then collapsed and was pronounced dead at

Flushing Hospital soon after. Four more members of the NYPD were injured, two critically.

Despite the largest manhunt in NYPD history up to that time, the bomber was never arrested or even identified, and the $26,000 reward for information never claimed.

## THE FAIR

The 1940 World's Fair, running from May 11 to October 27, was the second of the fair's two "seasons"; the first had opened on April 30, 1939, and ended about six months later. Home to both was a 1,202-acre fairground in Flushing Meadows–Corona Park, Queens, previously a malodorous dumping ground for the Brooklyn Ash Removal Company, which deposited fifty million cubic yards of garbage, ash, and animal carcasses there between 1910 and 1934. F. Scott Fitzgerald, whose commute from Long Island to Manhattan passed by the

WIKIMEDIA

swamp, described it in *The Great Gatsby* as a "valley of ashes—a fantastic farm where ashes grow like wheat into ridges and hills and grotesque gardens; where ashes take the forms of houses and chimneys and rising smoke and, finally, with a transcendent effort, of ash-grey men, who move dimly and already crumbling through the powdery air."

The fair cost $160 million to build, a staggering number for the time. The decades preceding had been blackened by World War I and the Great Depression, so it was no surprise that the World's Fair Corporation focused on the future, designating "Building the World of Tomorrow" as its theme. President Roosevelt touted the fair as a harbinger of better times: happiness, peace, and international goodwill. Not even close. While sixty-two nations built national halls or set up exhibitions, Germany bailed at the last minute; Adolf Hitler, sworn in as chancellor in 1933, had annexed Austria a year earlier and invaded Czechoslovakia on March 15.

"The rumble of German army caissons rolling into Prague echoed across the Flushing Meadows yesterday, where a $200,000 pavilion intended to house Czecho-Slovakia's exhibit at the New York World's Fair is nearing completion," the *New York Times* reported. "What will happen to the building, to the additional space reserved in the Hall of Nations by the Prague government and to the exhibits, some of which are already here, some en route and others on the docks at Hamburg, no one knew. The World's Fair now has a contract with a country that no longer exists."

World War II officially began on September 1, 1939, with Germany's invasion of Poland, and by the second season of the fair, several participating nations were mired in the conflict. The 1940 Summer Olympics (the "Phantom Olympics"), originally scheduled to take place in Tokyo but reassigned to Helsinki following the outbreak of the Sino-Japanese War in 1937, were eventually scrapped, after the November 1939 Soviet Union invasion of Finland. The 1940 season of the World's Fair nearly fell victim to hostilities as well—thirteen countries withdrew—though in the end the decision was made to proceed as planned.

But with a new theme: "For Peace and Freedom."

## THE BLAST

Marjorie Rossner was working the switchboard at the British Pavilion on Tuesday, July 2, when she received an anonymous call from a man with a German accent. A bomb's been planted inside the pavilion, the caller said. "Get everybody out of the building; it's going to blow up." Authorities were summoned, but a search turned up no sign of a bomb. Security was tightened. Detectives were assigned to mingle with visitors inside the building, on the lookout for anything suspicious. The Italian Pavilion, adjacent to the British exhibit, had received a postcard warning there would be an explosion on the premises that same day.

Nothing happened. But on the following day, during a casual inspection of the utility room in the British pavilion, electrician William Strachan discovered a buff-colored satchel about the size of an overnight bag. The third-floor room housed the air-conditioning unit, installed to protect valuable British artifacts from withering in the heat, and was off-limits to the general public. Strachan ignored the bag, thinking it belonged to one of the cleaning women. The following afternoon, he spotted it again. Now suspicious, he placed it to his ear and heard ticking. Gingerly, he threaded his way to the office of Cyril Rawlings, an assistant to the commissioner general. Rawlings called Sidney Grant Wood, chief of the uniformed police staff at the fair, who summoned Detectives Fred C. Morlock Jr. and William Federer. With the bag tucked under his arm, Morlock walked 1,600 feet through the crowd, finally depositing it on a grassy, isolated spot behind the Polish Pavilion. Authorities cordoned off the site and shooed everyone away.

All they could do now was wait for the NYPD bomb squad to arrive.

Detectives Joseph Lynch and Ferdinand "Freddy" Socha were relative newcomers to the elite, oddly conjoined six-man bomb and forgery squad. The thirty-three-year-old Lynch, described as "lantern jawed and handsome" by James Mauro in *Twilight at the World of Tomorrow*, came from a family of cops—both his father and older brother were on the force—but had nurtured different dreams: owning a neighborhood drugstore; a home in Riverdale, an upscale section of the Bronx; and a summer cottage by the beach. But he also had a wife and five kids, and confronted with the reality of the Great Depression, he chose instead the financial security of the NYPD and made do with a cramped two-bedroom apartment in the Kingsbridge neighborhood of the Bronx. Socha, from Greenpoint, Brooklyn, was two years older than Lynch and had five years more experience; round faced, with a receding hairline and double chin, he had studied medicine before joining the force.

Lynch was officially on duty on the Fourth but allowed to hang out at home as long as he made himself available should anything arise. At about 4:00 p.m., something did. Headquarters called informing him of the bomb threat at the fair. He dialed up Socha, who had the day off. Socha's wife answered, and when she told her husband the call was for him, he replied, "Tell them I'm not home." Informed it was Lynch, he took the call after all and agreed to accompany his partner to the fair.

**KILLED BY BOMB AT FAIR** were Detectives Ferdinand Socha (right) of Brooklyn and Joseph J. Lynch of the Bronx, both attached to the police Bomb and Forgery Squad.

PHOTO COURTESY OF THE *BROOKLYN EAGLE*

Earlier that year, the two had investigated a series of bomb threats in the city, including one just weeks earlier at the Italian Pavilion. All false alarms. Lynch told his wife, Easter, he'd be home in time for dinner, after which they would visit their daughter Essie, hospitalized in Yonkers with an infection in her bones. Lynch picked up Socha, and the partners headed for the fairgrounds.

By 5:00 p.m., they were crouching over the buff-colored fiber bag, measuring eighteen by twelve by six inches. This was before the era of bomb-sniffing dogs, sophisticated robots, or protective gear. Dressed in plain clothes, Lynch and Socha carefully lifted the satchel off the ground and examined it. Socha extracted a pocketknife and gingerly cut away a two-inch strip in the thin wooden veneer. Inside, they saw twelve sticks of dynamite connected to a timing device. A detective positioned close by, whose job it was to relay information from Lynch and Socha to the police commanders, asked Lynch what he saw.

"This looks like the real deal," Lynch responded.

Those were the last words he ever spoke.

Josephine Chmiel, a saleswoman at the Polish Pavilion candy counter, was looking out a window when the bomb went off. "It was a terrible explosion," she told reporters. "There were five men near the bomb when it went off. All of them were hit. Then three were lying down. Two were trying to crawl away, holding their faces. One tried to get to his feet. . . . Oh, it was horrible. I had to look away."

Captain John McLaughlin, of the World's Fair police department, who was standing about thirty-five feet away, said, "They were cutting the bag toward the bottom when Lynch turned around and said, 'This looks like the real goods.' When he said that, the others around him started to back away—took one or two steps. Then it went off. I was deafened by the explosion and blown back some feet."

## THE INVESTIGATION

According to Bernard Whalen, a former New York City police officer who has spent countless hours researching, writing, and speaking about the bombing, the NYPD launched the largest manhunt in its history to date immediately following the deaths of Lynch and Socha. Some nineteen thousand cops were mobilized. Mayor Fiorello La Guardia assured the public the killers would be apprehended. "Every man in the police department will remain on twenty-four-hour duty until this case is broken," he said. "This is one of the worst outrages this city has known. Whether it is the work of a crank or a radical makes little difference. We will not rest until the man or men responsible are captured and punished." Immunity was offered to anyone with valuable information. The police union put up $1,000, and the city added $25,000 in reward money—unclaimed to this day.

Beginning at the crack of dawn on July 5, police were sifting through the wreckage for clues, even examining the flesh of the victims. Recovered fragments were submitted to labs for examination by explosives experts. When a small piece of the satchel in which the bomb was contained was found, detectives fanned out in search of retailers who carried the brand. Particles of upholsterer's hair, used to cushion the explosive device, were found, rare enough that police were confident they could trace it. The timing device was an eight-day Ingraham clock; police looked for stores that sold them and customers who bought them. Police Commissioner Lee Valentine even ordered leaves stripped from the nearby maple tree that had been scorched by the blast to be raked and collected.

Not a single productive clue resulted from the search.

Hundreds of known "agitators"—including Communists; anarchists; Christian Fronters; Christian Mobilizers; and members of the Irish Republican Army and the German-American Bund, a pro-fascist German nationalist group—were rounded up for questioning, many subjected to what Whalen calls the "third degree," meaning some pretty nasty interrogation. The FBI lent a hand, though according to Whalen not a very vigorous one. "The FBI assigned an agent or two but never followed up on any leads," he said. At one point Whalen asked the FBI for information on the case and was told no such files existed.

Initial suspicion centered on Nazi sympathizers, especially the German-American Bund, formed in 1936 by Fritz Julius Kuhn, the self-described "American Fuhrer," to promote German interests. The Bund was hyperactive in the late thirties, organizing marches and demonstrations at which participants—many of them German immigrants—waved swastika banners, including an infamous rally at Madison Square Garden in February 1939 where twenty thousand Nazi sympathizers chanted "Heil Hitler." The Bund also ran more than a dozen summer camps similar to Hitler Youth Camps, including Camp Siegfried in Yaphank, New York, which ran its own train on the Long Island Railroad during the summer, nicknamed the "Camp Siegfried Special." Campers, dressed in Hitler Youth uniforms and carrying Nazi banners, attended shooting drills and classes on survivalism and eugenics.

The rallies and camps drew increasingly hostile protests from anti-German groups as tensions rose throughout the city. Thousands of anti-Nazi demonstrators gathered outside Madison Square Garden during the 1939 rally. When Jewish protestor Isadore Greenbaum slipped inside and rushed the stage, which was adorned with photos of Hitler and George Washington, storm troopers attacked him. On June 20, 1940, a bomb ripped apart the offices of the Communist Party USA's *Daily Worker* at 35 East Twelfth Street. That same day, a time bomb exploded at 17 Battery Place, home of the German Consulate. On June 21, a caller informed Manhattan police the Bund was planning to blow up the Brooklyn Bridge.

Not a single person was ever charged in connection with the bombing. Police did arrest thirty-eight-year-old Caesar Kroeger (aka Caesar Kroger aka

Edward Kangesier), a member of the German-American Bund, after discovering two German-made pistols, one loaded, inside his apartment, under a copy of Hitler's *Mein Kampf.* On the wall they found a huge world map, marked with chalk and pins on major US cities, which Kroeger said represented the locations of Communist units. He was held on charges of violating gun laws, but nothing else.

Pro-German fascists weren't the only suspects. Some authorities suspected the Irish Republican Army was behind the blast. Others wondered if French nationals might have sought revenge for Britain's "sucker punch" just twenty-four hours earlier: a sneak bombing attack on Vichy France's naval fleet, intended to keep the ships from falling into German hands and resulting in 1,300 fatalities. With Russia's Joseph Stalin having signed a nonaggression pact with Hitler, members of both the Communist Party and anti-Communist groups were hauled in for questioning.

John F. Cassidy, a Christian Fronter and acolyte of popular radio priest, virulent anti-Semite, and thinly veiled Hitler fanatic Father Charles Coughlin, was among the many rabid anti-Communists questioned; Cassidy wrote about the experience for the July 13 issue of *The Tablet*, a Catholic newspaper published by a subsidiary of the Diocese of Brooklyn. He had been among the eighteen men arrested on January 13, 1940, on charges of attempting to overthrow the government, with the ultimate goal of setting up a Hitler-like dictatorship (Cassidy eventually was acquitted). FBI Director J. Edgar Hoover charged that the group had planned to blow up the *Jewish Daily Forward* newspaper office, the Cameo Theater on West Forty-second Street (which showed Russian-made films), the General Post Office, and the Federal Reserve Bank. When the FBI arrested the club's core members, it confiscated fifteen bombs, eighteen cans of cordite powder, twelve Springfield rifles, four .22-caliber rifles, 750 rounds of machine-gun ammunition, dynamite, fuses, incendiary chemicals, and a long sword.

"With reference to the bombing, I consider it a most hideous thing, and regret that the unfortunate policemen who appeared on the scene lost their lives in a war that foreigners have brought to our city, while we are spending every house of our energy to KEEP AMERICA OUT OF THE WAR AND TO KEEP THE WAR OUT OF AMERICA," Cassidy wrote. "I trust that God will shed light on the real culprits and that they will be brought to justice for this crime against the victims and against our country as a whole."

Police also pondered the possibility that the explosion was connected to the theft of thirty-nine sticks of dynamite at gunpoint on May 29 for a synagogue excavation on West Sixty-eighth Street. They followed up on a lead from

R. C. Rosser, the husband of the British Pavilion telephone operator who had answered the bomb threat on July 2, who told police he had received a call at home from a man who told him in a muffled voice, "I'll kill you," then hung up. And they briefly considered, then rejected, the possibility that the explosion was the handiwork of the Mad Bomber of New York, George Peter Metesky, who terrorized the city over a sixteen-year period beginning in November 1940, with explosives planted in transportation hubs and landmark city buildings, before being apprehended in 1957.

Could the bomb have been a false flag planted by agents of the British government so that Hitler's supporters would be blamed? Both Germany and Great Britain were angling to influence American opinion: Britain wanted the United States to join the fight against the Axis powers; Germany wanted it to stay the hell out. Hitler was prepping a cross-Channel invasion; the Battle of Britain would begin on July 10. Exactly a month before the bombing, the British had evacuated their entire army from Europe after retreating to Dunkirk. According to the *New York Times*, the Brits were so strapped for cash that they too had nearly pulled out of the 1940 season of the World's Fair: "The British Pavilion at the New York World's Fair will reopen this year if Grover Whalen, president of the Fair Corporation, can figure out a way to save the British Government the $250,000 it would cost to operate it, it was understood today. The question is whether the government can afford to spend that much money on its pavilion when it needs all its money for the war."

Could the British have been behind the bombing? It's a popular theory. Soon after the explosion, NYPD Police Commissioner Lew Valentine opined that only someone who worked in the British Pavilion or was intimately familiar with the building's plans could have known enough about the structure to plant the bomb in the strategic spot in which it was found. Bernard Whalen also believes the British might have been behind it; his suspicions were reaffirmed when he read the police files on the investigation: The NYPD was prohibited from speaking to security staff at the British Pavilion without permission, which wasn't easy to obtain. "If I wanted to solve a crime, I wouldn't impede investigators in any shape or form," he said. "It could have just been the stuffy British attitude, but the authorities at the pavilion were interfering."

Just weeks before the bombing, Winston Churchill had dispatched Sir William Stephenson, a World War I hero code-named Intrepid, to New York to set up an MI6 office with the purpose of coaxing the United States to enter the war. One of Stephenson's agents was Ian Fleming, who later modeled his James Bond character on his boss, a man he described as "very tough, very rich, single-minded, patriotic, and a man of few words." (A fighter pilot during World War I and a self-made millionaire, Stephenson at one point volunteered to assassinate Hitler, though the plan was eventually scrapped.)

*NY City Lens*'s Matthew Benedetti reported that in 1999, newly declassified documents released by the United Kingdom National Archives revealed the "breathtaking scale and scope of the espionage and propaganda operations conducted by [Stephenson's British Security Coordination] in the United States," including blackmail campaigns against isolationist government officials.

### THE AFTERMATH

According to Whalen, when the parish priest appeared at the Lynch house to inform the officer's wife of her husband's death, "she assumed the worst because she had seen that look on a pastor's face before. Three years earlier, her mother had been murdered in the family grocery store." Easter called the hospital where their daughter Essie, ten years old at the time, was being treated and instructed staff there to keep her away from the radio. By phone, she then told Essie that her father had left on a business trip; it would be another month before she learned the truth.

Before the start of the 1964 World's Fair at the same site in Flushing Meadows Park, a plaque and stone marker were dedicated to Lynch and Socha. Years later, it was moved to its current site, a garden alongside the Queens Museum, which had served as the New York Pavilion in 1940, the last original structure remaining from the 1939–1940 New York World's Fair.

On July 11, 2015, on the seventy-fifth anniversary of the bombing, a memorial service was held at the site of the plaque, assembled by the New York Police Department's bomb squad. According to Whalen, the NYPD keeps a photograph of the reconstruction of the satchel made as part of the investigation hanging in the hallway outside the chief of detectives' office at police headquarters, a reminder of the sacrifice made by Lynch and Socha.

In 2013, Lynch and Socha made cameo appearances in the comic book series *The Shadow/Green Hornet: Dark Nights*, written by Michael Uslan and illustrated by Keith Burns (even if the bombing is inaccurately portrayed as having happened in 1939 rather than 1940). The bomber here is Shiwan Khan, descendant of Genghis and no slouch in the "I'm-gonna-conquer-the-world" department either. Khan, aligned with Hitler, defends the bombing as a "dire warning to your country to stay out of conflicts that are none of your business." "Those two brave men sacrificed themselves for us. But not in vain . . . I swear not in vain," one of our heroes says (they are drawn in such a way in this sequence that it is hard to tell which is which). "Those two men were the first casualties in a world war America is already in, but not yet willing to fight." "Those two policemen will be remembered. They will be avenged," the Shadow says.

When the 1940 World's Fair shuttered for good on October 27, the *New York Times* eulogized it thusly: "On the tombstone of the Flushing giant should be carved something like this: 'Born, April 30, 1939. Passed away officially at midnight, October 27, 1940. A short life—and not always a merry one.'"

# Acknowledgments

First, thanks to Kate Ayers, Greta Schmitz, Meredith Dias, Anthony Pomes, Karen Weldon, Neil Cotterill, Ann Seifert, and Susan Barnett at Globe Pequot for their support.

Many, many people and places assisted in the research for and writing of this book, and we extend our extreme gratitude to all of them, including:

Elizabeth Applebaum, the New England History Society (Leslie Landrigan, Nina Brown, and Howard Brown), Justin Peavey, James Polchin, the Westchester County Archives (Jackie Graziano), and Bernard Whalen.

Special thanks to our old friend John Walsh, who left us one last gift in the form of an old email about a family brutally murdered on a farm near his home in Sand Lake, many decades ago. R.I.P., John.

Thanks also to the New York chapter of the Mystery Writers of America for affording us an opportunity to present an excerpt from this book at a public reading.

David also thanks the three most important people in his life for their love and support: Mariam, Alex, and Scout.

Mark, as always, expresses gratitude and love to his family: Tara, Felix, Greta, Reggie (and Ivory!). He would also like to thank Elizabeth "Betsy" Foster for always being there over the years, and especially for the piles of Sherlock Holmes on VHS in the summer countryside.

# Bibliography

## Chapter 1: Who Wants to Kill a Millionaire?
"Frightful Tragedy in New York." *The Brooklyn Daily Times*. July 29, 1870
"The Nathan Tragedy." *The Brooklyn Daily Times*. July 30, 1870.
"Assassination of a Prominent Broker of New York." *Brooklyn Eagle*. July 30, 1870.
"The Nathan Assassination Case." *The Buffalo Daily Republic*. July 30, 1870.
"Murdered for Gold." *New York Daily Herald*. July 30, 1870.
"Benjamin Nathan, the Broker, Assassinated in His Own House." *The New York Times*. July 30, 1870.
"The Mysterious Murder." *New York Daily Herald*. July 31, 1870.
"The Nathan Murder." *New York Tribune*. August 1, 1870.
"Mr. Nathan's Murderer." *The Sun*. August 1, 1870.
"The Nathan Murder." *New York Daily Herald*. August 2, 1870.
"The Nathan Horror." *New York Daily Herald*. August 3, 1870.
"The Nathan Mystery." *New York Daily Herald*. August 7, 1870.
"The Nathan Horror." *New York Daily Herald*. August 8, 1870.
"The Nathan Murder." *New York Daily Herald*. August 10, 1870.
"The Nathan Inquest." *New York Tribune*. September 15, 1870. https://www.tabletmag.com/sections/community/articles/a-death-in-the-family.

## Chapter 2: The New York Ripper
"Many Arrests: But No Identification of 'Jack the Ripper.'" *The Brooklyn Daily Eagle*. April 25, 1891.
"'Ripper's Victim Slain by Lunatic, Autopsy Shows." *The Evening World*. March 20, 1915.
"Clews in Murder Point to 'Friend' as Child Slayer." *New-York Tribune*. March 21, 1915.
"Child Victim of 'Ripper' Is Carried to Her Grave as Women Crowd Street." *The Evening World*. March 22, 1915.
"Arrest Near Scene of Child's Murder." *The New York Times*. March 23, 1915.
"Police Seek Man in House as Suspect in 'Ripper' Case." *The Evening World*. March 23, 1915.
"The City Mother's Load of Terror." *The New York Times*. March 27, 1915.
"Mother of Slain Girl Threatened in 'Ripper' Note." *The Evening World*. March 29, 1915.
"Child's Mother Receives Fresh 'Ripper' Threats." *The Evening World*. March 31, 1915.
"Boy Murdered by East Side 'Ripper.'" *The New York Times*. May 4, 1915.

"Girl Escaped Ripper Before He Killed Boy." *New-York Tribune.* May 5, 1915.
"Ripper Note Sent to Boy's Funeral Says 'Kill Again.'" *The Sun.* May 7, 1915.
"Trying to Trap 'Ripper'; Children Parade Streets with Hidden Guards Near." *The Evening World.* May 8, 1915.
"Philadelphia 'Ripper' a Puzzle; 'Innocent,' Says One Mother." *New-York Tribune,* June 24, 1915.
"'Ripper' Is Trapped Says Man Who Wove Mesh About Killer." *Brooklyn Eagle.* July 25, 1915.
"'Ripper' Suspect Denies Murders; Woman Accuses." *The Evening World.* August 17, 1915.
"Police Sceptical of Ripper Story." *The Sun.* August 18, 1915.
"Police in Cruger Case Removed." *The New York Times.* June 21, 1917.
"Cocchi Arrested, Will Fight Trial Here for Murder." *The New York Times.* June 23, 1917.
"Cocchi Confesses; Slew Ruth Cruger for Repelling Him." *The New York Times.* June 24, 1917.
"Police Were Deaf to Pleas of Sister." *The New York Times.* June 26, 1917.
"Cocchi Tells How He Slew Ruth Criger." *The New York Times.* June 26, 1917.
"Wallstein Finds Gross Neglect in Cocci Case." *The New York Times.* June 27, 1917.
Asbury, Herbert. *The Gangs of New York: An Informal History of the Underworld.* Alfred A. Knopf, Inc., 1927.
Jones, Richard. "The Murder of Carrie Brown." Jack the Ripper Tour, August 25, 2019. https://www.jack-the-ripper-tour.com/generalnews/the-murder-of-carrie-brown/.
Morley, Christopher J. *Jack the Ripper Suspects.* Independently published, 2023.
Brown, Howard, and Nina Brown. *An Illustrated Encyclopedia: The 1891 Murder of Carrie.* Independently published, 2025.

## CHAPTER 3: WHO IS BURIED IN GREENFIELD CEMETERY?
"Suicide at Hempstead." *Brooklyn Daily Times.* April 12, 1904.
"Woman's Body Found in Woods Near Freeport." *Brooklyn Eagle.* April 12, 1904.
"Found Woman Dead in Woods." *The New York Times.* April 12, 1904.
"Murder, Not Suicide, Theory in Freeport Case." *Brooklyn Eagle.* April 13, 1904.
"Mystery at Freeport Is yet to Be Solved." *Brooklyn Eagle.* April 14, 1904.
"Woman Slain Says Justice." *The Evening World.* April 14, 1904.
"Mystery May Involve Rich New York Man." *Buffalo News.* April 15, 1904.
"Murder May Be Solution of the Freeport Mystery." *Brooklyn Eagle.* April 17, 1904.
"Tale of Body Snatchers at Freeport Is Doubted." *Brooklyn Daily Times.* April 19, 1904.
"Woman's Burial Held Up." *The New York Times.* April 19, 1904.
"Freeport Mystery Is as Mysterious as Ever." *Brooklyn Daily Times.* April 20, 1904.
"Clue to Freeport Mystery." *The New York Times.* April 20, 1904.
"Watch Brooklyn Man." *New York Tribune.* April 20, 1904.
"Buried as Martha Laimbeer." *The Sun.* April 20, 1904.
"Woman Swallowed Acid." *The New York Times.* April 23, 1904.
"Brooklyn Man Murder Suspect." *Brooklyn Citizen.* September 11, 1904.
"Thinks Woman Murdered." *New York Tribune.* September 11, 1904.

## Bibliography

"Reopened Old 'Suicide' Case." *The New York Times*. September 11, 1904.
"Says Pen Solves Murder Mystery." *The Evening World*. September 12, 1904.
"Authorities on Track of Girl's Murderer." *Brooklyn Citizen*. September 16, 1904.
"Sensation Due in Woods Mystery." *The Evening World*. September 16, 1904.
"Solving Cemetery Mystery May Result in Sensation." *Brooklyn Eagle*. September 17, 1904.
"Arrest Is Expected Soon in Freeport Murder Case." *Brooklyn Citizen*. September 18, 1904.
"Lynch Girl a Suicide Says Parish Priest." *Brooklyn Citizen*. September 20, 1904.
"No Greenfield Mystery; Miss Lynch the Suicide." *Brooklyn Eagle*. September 20, 1904.
"False Clue Reveals New Death Mystery." *The Evening World*. September 20, 1904.
"Freeport Suicide Brooklyn Girl." *The Times Union*. September 20, 1904.
"Lynch Girl's Body Taken to Woods, Priest Says." *Brooklyn Citizen*. September 21, 1904.
"Was It Miss Lynch's Body?" *Brooklyn Daily Times*. September 21, 1904.
"Margaret Lynch's Friend Defends Dead Girl's Name." *Brooklyn Eagle*. September 21, 1904.
"May Not Be Lynch Girl." *The New York Times*. September 21, 1904.
"Doubts If Lynch Girl Was Freeport Suicide." *The Times Union*. September 21, 1904.
"Miss Lynch Was Self Slain." *The Sun*. September 21, 1904.
"Family of Miss Lynch Accuse the Elder Maune." *Brooklyn Eagle*. September 22, 1904.
"Will Summon Maune to "Laimbeer" Inquest." *Brooklyn Citizen*. September 23, 1904.
"Maune Not to Be Found; Lynch Case at a Halt." *Brooklyn Eagle*. September 24, 1904.
"Dr. Shay Was the Dentist." *Brooklyn Eagle*. September 25, 1904.
"Will Dig Up Girl's Body." *New York Tribune*. September 27, 1904.
"Lynch Girl Murdered, Authorities Insist." *Brooklyn Citizen*. September 28, 1904.
"Talk of an Accomplice as Freeport Murderer." *Brooklyn Daily Times*. September 28, 1904.
"Identify Miss Lynch." *New York Tribune*. September 28, 1904.
"District Attorney Will Visit Maune." *The Evening World*. September 29, 1904.
"Think Lynch Girl Slain." *The Post Star*. September 29, 1904.
"Closing Chapter in Lynch Girl's Story." *The Evening World*. October 4, 1904.
"Justice Wallace Insists Margaret Lynch Is Alive." *Brooklyn Eagle*. October 12, 1904.
"Coroner Hears That Miss Lynch Is Alive." *The Times Union*. October 12, 1904.
"Coroner to Resume Inquest in Lynch Case." *Brooklyn Eagle*. October 19, 1904.
"Lynch Inquest Resumed; New Witness Appears." *Brooklyn Citizen*. October 21, 1904.
"Lynch Girl Tried to Die in Park." *The Evening World*. October 21, 1904.
"Grief for Dead Sister Hastened Lynch's Death." *Brooklyn Eagle*. October 25, 1904.
"Lynch Inquest Resumed." *Brooklyn Eagle*. October 28, 1904.
"Friendliness of Maune with Miss Lynch Shown." *Brooklyn Citizen*. October 29, 1904.
"Margaret Lynch's Body, Says Dentist Jon F. Shea." *Brooklyn Daily Times*. October 29, 1904.
"Mrs. Lynch on the Stand." *Brooklyn Eagle*. November 1, 1904.
"Mother of Lynch Girl Testifies." *The Evening World*. November 1, 1904.
"Facts Point to Suicide in Margaret Lynch Case." *Brooklyn Daily Times*. November 2, 1904.

"Lynch Family's Ordeal at Coroner's Inquest." *Brooklyn Eagle*. November 2, 1904.
"Read Lynch Girl's Note." *New York Tribune*. November 2, 1904.
"Margaret Lynch Inquest." *Brooklyn Daily Times*. November 29, 1904.
"Maune, Sr., Not There." *New York Tribune*. December 3, 1904.
"Wallace Says the Girl Was Not Margaret Lynch." *Brooklyn Eagle*. November 17, 1905.
"Famous Tragedies That Balked Solution." *Fresno Morning Republican*. April 14, 1912.

## CHAPTER 4: A LADY VANISHES

"Girl Seeking Disguise May Be Lost Heiress." *The Evening World*. January 26, 1911.
"Ransom of $5000 for Vanished Girl Demand on Father." *The Evening World*. January 27, 1911.
"Find Clew to Girl." *The Washington Post*. January 27, 1911.
"Long Missing Girl Read Foreign Letter, Joined Man, Vanished." *The Evening World*. January 28, 1911.
"Dorothy Arnold May Be Home To-Day." *The New York Times*. January 28, 1911.
"Girl Still Missing." *The Washington Post*. January 28, 1911.
"Silence of Death, Says Girl's Father." *The New York Times*. January 29, 1911.
"Clews to Girl Fail." *The Washington Post*. January 29, 1911.
"Arnold Girl's Parents Appeal to Government to Help Find Daughter." *The Evening World*. January 30, 1911.
"Arnolds Tell All of Search for Girl." *The New York Times*. January 30, 1911.
"Believe Girl in Lake." *The Washington Post*. January 30, 1911.
"Dorothy Arnold Dead, Her Relatives Declare; Mother Scours Europe." *The Evening World*. January 31, 1911.
"Mrs. Arnold May Be Seeking Girl Abroad." *The New York Times*. January 31, 1911.
"Says Heiress Is Safe." *The Washington Post*. January 31, 1911.
"Dorothy Arnold Vanished Before from Her Home." *The Evening World*. February 1, 1911.
"Deny Miss Arnold Went Away by Boat." *The New York Times*. February 1, 1911.
"Hunting Heiress Here." *The Washington Post*. February 1, 1911.
"Dorothy Arnold Quarreled with Father and Fled." *The Evening World*. February 2, 1911.
"Sought Miss Arnold Last Thanksgiving." *The New York Times*. February 2, 1911.
"Denials by Griscom." *The Washington Post*. February 2, 1911.
"Dorothy Arnold Sailed for Italy in January, Latest Clue in Search." *The Evening World*. February 3, 1911.
"Seek Miss Arnold in Philadelphia." *The New York Times*. February 3, 1911.
"Heiress Was Unhappy." *The Washington Post*. February 3, 1911.
"Dorothy Arnold Hiding in Quaker City Suburbs; Clue to Missing Girl." *The Evening World*. February 4, 1911.
"Dorothy Arnold Not in Philadelphia." *The New York Times*. February 4, 1911.
"Missing Girl Reported." *The Washington Post*. February 4, 1911.
"Arnold Girl Gone Now Fifty-Five Days." *The New York Times*. February 5, 1911.
"Hunt for Arnold Girl Again Leads to Philadelphia." *The Evening World*. February 6, 1911.

"No Clue to Girl, Arnolds Declare." *The New York Times*. February 6, 1911.
"Foil Griscom's Plan to Meet Arnold Girl and Maker Her Bride." *The Evening World*. February 14, 1911.
"Miss Arnold Seen in Florence, Girl Writes Her Sister." *The Evening World*. March 3, 1911.

## CHAPTER 5: FARMHOUSE TRAGEDY

"Three Murdered Bodies Found in Manure Pit." *Bennington Banner*. December 14, 1911.
"Horrible Murders." *Biddeford-Saco Journal*. December 14, 1911.
"Four Headless Bodies Found!" *Buffalo Inquirer*. December 14, 1911.
"Women Murdered Hid in Manure." *Daily Sentinel*. December 14, 1911.
"Slayer of Four in Family, In Flight from Albany, Sought by Police Here." *The Evening World*. December 14, 1911.
"Horrible Murder of Four Discovered Near Albany." *Press and Sunday Bulletin*. December 14, 1911.
"Morner Murder Fugitive Hunted; Two Men Arrested." *The Evening World*. December 15, 1911.
"Bloodhounds Trail Slayer of Family." *The New York Times*. December 15, 1911.
"4 Bodies Under Barn Floor." *The Sun*. December 15, 1911.
"Police Hope to Find Murderer of 4 Soon." *The Tribune*. December 15, 1911.
"Morner Murder Suspect Is Held at Porchester." *The Evening World*. December 16, 1911.
"State May Offer Reward for Slayer." *The Evening World*. December 17, 1911.
"Dix May Offer Reward." *The Tribune*. December 17, 1911.
"Blood on the Door of Morner Suspect." *The New York Times*. December 19, 1911.
"Looks Bad for Donato." *The Tribune*. December 19, 1911.
"Not the Morners' Slayer." *The New York Times*. January 4, 1912.
"Caught as Slayer of Whole Family on Farm." *The Evening World*. March 1, 1912.

## CHAPTER 6: A BRIDGE TOO FAR

"Seek Young Woman in Elwell Mystery." *The New York Times*. June 13, 1920.
"Scour City Garages for Elwell Clue." *The New York Times*. June 14, 1920.
"'Woman in Black' at the Ritz Enters Elwell Mystery." *The New York Times*. June 16, 1920.
"Housekeeper Admits Shielding Woman by Hiding Garments in Elwell Home; Now Breaks Down and Reveals Her Name." *The New York Times*. June 17, 1920.
"Mrs. Elwell Bares Divorce Project." *The New York Times*. June 17, 1920.
"Von Schlegell Again Questioned in Mystery." *The Evening World*. June 17, 1920.
"Viola Kraus and Ex-Husband Again on Elwell Grill." *The New York Times*. June 18, 1920.
"Swann Baffled at Every Turn in Elwell Mystery." *The New York Times*. June 19, 1920.
"Elwell, the Man of Many Masks." *The New York Times*. June 20, 1920.
"Elwell, Discarding Palm Beach Woman, Revealed Threats." *The New York Times*. June 20, 1920.
"'Woman in Gray' Sought as Elwell Mystery Clears." *Daily News*. June 21, 1920.
"Woman in Gray Sought in Murder of Elwell." *New-York Tribune*. June 21, 1920.

"'Unwritten Law' Avenger Sought in Elwell Case." *The New York Times*. June 22, 1920.
"Girl in Black Will Return to Tell Story." *The Brooklyn Daily Times*. June 23, 1920.
"Housekeeper Gives New Elwell Facts." *The New York Times*. June 25, 1920.
"Dooling on Secret Hunt in Elwell Murder Case After Finding New Clue." *The Evening World*. June 25, 1920.
"All Elwell Clues Center on a Man, Arrest Expected." *The New York Times*. June 26, 1920.
"Whole Thing a Fiasco, Elwell's Friend Says." *St. Louis Post-Dispatch*. June 28, 1920.
"'Bootlegger' Clue in Elwell Case Bared by Check." *The New York Times*. June 29, 1920.
"U.S. Agents Sift Elwell Rum Clue." *The New York Times*. June 30, 1920.
"Elwell 'Bootlet' Clue Collapses." *The New York Times*. July 1, 1920.
"Elwell Rum Ring Bared by Shevlin." *The New York Times*. July 2, 1920.
"Pendleton's Alibi in Elwell Mystery Attacked by Swann." *The New York Times*. July 8, 1920.
"Friends Confirm Pendleton Story." *The New York Times*. July 9, 1920.
"Whiskey Is Seized in Elwell Mystery." *The New York Times*. July 10, 1920.
"Elwell Evidence Put Up to Whitman." *The New York Times*. April 2, 1921.
"Hired by Woman to Kill Elwell." *Boston Daily Glove*. April 7, 1921.
"Experts Find Harris Is Sane; N.Y. Says House Plan Correct." *The Buffalo Enquirer*. April 7, 1921.
"Higgins Believes Confession True." *The Buffalo Times*. April 7, 1921.
"Confessed Elwell Slayer Identifies Woman Employer." *The New York Times*. April 8, 1921.
"Elwell Confessions Forced, Says Harris." *The Evening Sun*. April 8, 1921.
"Whitman Refuses to Arrest Woman." *The New York Times*. April 8, 2921.
"Harris Sticks to Story Pal Slew Elwell; New York Officers Think Confession Fake." *Buffalo Courier Express*. April 8, 1921.
Goodman, Jonathan. *The Slaying of Joseph Bowne Elwell*. Harrap, 1987.

## Chapter 7: The Sailor, the Baker, the Westchester Head Shaker

"Police Still Seek Backing for Ward's Self-Defense Please." *The New York Times*. May 24, 1922.
Whittaker, James. "Photos of Women Furnish Clew to Motive for Ward Slaying." *Daily News*. May 24, 1922.
"Peters Killed by Walter S. Ward to Shield Another Man, Is Report." *The Evening World*. May 26, 1922.
"Ward Sent to Jail for Peters' Killing; Grand Jury's Order." *The New York Herald*. May 26, 1922.
Whittaker, James. "Ward Rearrested on Court Order; Spends Night in Cell." *Daily News*. May 26, 1922.
"Ward Rearrested, Dines with Sheriff But Sleeps in Jail." *The New York Times*. May 26, 1922.
"Ward Loses Fight for Release, But Keeps His Secret." *The New York Times*. May 27, 1922.

Whittaker, James. "Charlie Ross in Ward Case Identified by News." *Daily News*. May 27, 1922.
Whittaker, James. "Arrest of Second Ward Blackmailer Nears." *Daily News*. May 28, 1922.
Whittaker, James. "Ward Menaced with New Blackmail as 'Ross' Flees." *Daily News*. May 29, 1922.
Whittaker, James. "Fallon Again Fails to Produce Ross in Ward Case." *Daily News*. May 30, 1922.
"Ward Blackmailed Before Over a Girl; $1,000 Hushed Case." *The New York Times*. May 30, 1922.
Whittaker, James. "'Ross' Found by News, Gives Perfect Alibi in Ward Mystery." *Daily News*. May 31, 1922.
"Weeks as Witness Disqualified from Prosecuting Ward." *The New York Herald*. June 1, 1922.
"Ward to Be Faced by Cunningham in Murder Story Test." *The New York Herald*. June 3, 1922.
"Cunningham Faces Ward, Says 'Hello!' But Is Repudiated." *The New York Times*. June 6, 1922.
"Women May Clear Blackmail Story." *The Baltimore Sun*. June 23, 1922.
"Doyle Wants Spook Put on Ward Trail." *The New York Times*. June 25, 1922.
"Lawyers to Fight Today to Bail Ward." *The New York Herald*. June 26, 1922.
"Ward Weighs Justice Scales." *Daily News*. January 3, 1923.
Cowan, Joseph A. "Inquiry Axe Hits in Ward Case." *Daily News*. April 3, 1923.
"Gun Given Ward by Police Chief Linked in Probe." *Daily News*. April 7, 1923.
"Is Justice Broke?" *Daily News*. April 28, 1923.
"Paid Witnesses Turn on Ward." *Daily News*. April 29, 1923.
"Ward Denial of Killing Hinted." *Daily News*. May 2, 1923.
"Court Still Shields Ward Telegrams." *Daily News*. May 3, 1923.
"Stain Erased from Ward Victim." *Daily News*. May 4, 1923.
"Jury Inquiry in Ward Case." *Daily News*. May 26, 1923.
Cowan, Joseph. "New York Judge for Ward Case." *Daily News*. May 27, 1923.
"What Has Happened to Justice?" *Daily News*. June 10, 1923.
"Lobbying Against Justice." *Daily News*. July 11, 1923.
"Proof to State of Witness Gag in Ward Defense." *Daily News*. August 9, 1923.
"Court Refused Stay Against Ward Ruling." *Daily News*. August 15, 1923.
"Mills Pleads for Ward's Life." *Daily News*. September 27, 1923.
"Ward's Lawyers Get Grand Jury Rebuke." *Daily News*. October 5, 1923.
Polchin, James. *Shadow Men: The Tangled Story of Murder, Media, and Privilege That Scandalized Jazz Age America*. Counterpoint, 2024.

## CHAPTER 8: LOCKED AND LOADED

"Harlem Man Is Found Shot Dead by Assailant Who Entered Through Transom." *The New York Times*. March 10, 1929.
"Perfect Plot: New York Police Can't Solve Riddle of Murder of Laundryman." *Pittsburgh Press*. March 11, 1929.

"N.Y. Police Detectives Are Baffled by 'Perfect Crime.'" *Long Beach Sun*. March 11, 1929.
Antheil, George. "Boy Advises Girl: A Column for Modern Women." *Lexington Herald-Leader*. December 3, 1938.
Applebaum, Elizabeth. "The Mysterious Death of Mr. Fink." *The Detroit Jewish News*. August 15, 1997.
"How Was a Man Shot to Death Inside a Locked Shop . . . With No Gun?" *The New York Times*. n.d.
Penzler, Otto. "The Locked Room Mysteries: As a New Collection of the Genre's Best Published, Its Editor Otto Penzler Explains the Rules of Engagement." *The Independent*. December 28, 2014.
Brooks, C. C. "Isidore Fink: A Real-Life 'Locked Room Mystery.'" HubPages. September 5, 2023.

## Chapter 9: Who Ordered the Cement Shoes?

"Chauffeur Held after Raid on Bank." *New York Times*. July 9, 1920.
"Severest Sentence for Unlicensed Autoist." *Daily News*. January 29, 1921.
"Abe Weinberg Gets 60-Day Sentence." *Daily News*. April 12, 1933.
"Next, U.S. Goes After Beer Baron Schultz." *Daily News*. December 10, 1933.
"Link Schultz to $1,500,000 at U.S. Trial" *Daily News*. April 18, 1935.
"State to End Tracing of Schultz Banking." *Washington Daily News*. April 18, 1935.
"Missing Schultz Aid, Bo Weinberg Is Feared Slain." *Daily News*. September 24, 1935.
"Dutch Seized in Mysterious Move in N.J." *Daily News*. September 26, 1935.
"Bride Afraid Rivals Killed Schultz Ally." *Daily News*. September 28, 1935.
"Cops Fear Gang War Over Amberg Slaying." *Daily News*. October 2, 1935.
"Gang Wars of New York." *Daily News*. October 25, 1935.
"Dutch Had Wife 3; Hid Riches for Her." *Daily News*. October 27, 1935.
"Investigators Link Torrio to Schultz Death." *Daily News*. October 28, 1935.
"Secret Schultz Rites Foil Morbid Crowds." *Daily News*. October 29, 1935.
"Get 'Big 6' in Schultz Job, Mayor's Edict." *Daily News*. October 30, 1935.
"Police Hunt Missing Legal Aid of Schultz." *Daily News*. November 4, 1935.
"Slaying Gives Clut to Fate of Weinberg." *Daily News*. November 5, 1935.
"Link Sherman to Killing of Schultz Gang." *Daily News*. November 6, 1935.
"Schultz Pal Accused by Dutch's Widow." *Daily News*. November 7, 1935.
"U.S. Trust Law Brings Gurrah, Lepke to Trial." *Daily News*. October 27, 1936.
"Showgirl's Marriage to Schultz Aid Annuled." *Daily News*. April 18, 1937.
"30 Policy Killings Bared as Two Sob for Bail Reduction." *Daily News*. July 16, 1937.
"Bo Weinberg's Ex Is Wed to Movie Actor." *Daily News*. July 20, 1937.
"Dixie Davis Trapped in Phila. Love Nest; $300,00 Bail Set." *Daily News*. February 3, 1938.
"Crime Saga." *Daily News*. February 4, 1938.
"Dixie Davis Grilled in Torrio Tax Inquiry." *Daily News*. March 31, 1938.
"Dewey Seizes Hines as Policy Ring Head." *Daily News*. May 26, 1938.
"Dewey Brands Hines Schultz Ring Brain; Hints 6 Will Squeal." *Daily News*. May 27, 1938.

"Policy Banker Is State's First Witness." *Daily News*. August 18, 1938.
"Crime Corporation." *Daily News*. April 7, 1940.
"5-And-10 Murder." *El Paso Times*. April 21, 1940.
"Broadway Varieties." *The Republican*. March 1, 1941.
"Men and Maids—and Stuff." *Daily News*. May 5, 1941.
"Seen and Heard." *Democrat and Chronicle*. February 15, 1964.
Sann, Paul. *Kill The Dutchman!* Arlington House, 1971.
"Miserly and Murderous." *The Times* (Louisiana). November 4, 1982.
Dutch Schultz—The Most Ruthless Mob Boss of Them All. https://www.youtube.com/watch?v=7GXkheeh0eE&t=5303s.
Mad Dog Coll—The Most Feared & Hated Mobster in New York. https://www.youtube.com/watch?v=PdCeBABn0GE.

## CHAPTER 10: THE BOMB HEARD 'ROUND THE WORLD'S FAIR

Fitzgerald, F. Scott. *The Great Gatsby*. Scribner's Sons, 1925.
"Czech Fair Is Now an Orphan." *The New York Times*. March 17, 1939.
"Britain Hopes to Open Its Pavilion." *The New York Times*. February 22, 1940.
"Bomb Planted in British Pavilion at Fair Kills 2." *Daily News*. July 5, 1940.
"New York: Death at the Fair." *Time*. July 15, 1940.
Whalen, Bernard. "Easter Lynch." Spring 3100: The Magazine for the Department by the Department. 2002.
Mauro, James. *Twilight at the World of Tomorrow: Genius, Madness, Murder, and the 1939 World's Fair on the Brink of War*. Ballantine Books, 2010.
Uslan, Michael, and Keith Burns (illustrator). *The Shadow/Green Hornet: Dark Knights Volumes1–5*. Dynamite Entertainment, 2013.
"Did Brits Kill New York City Cops to Get U.S. into WWII." *Daily Beast*. July 16, 2017.
Whalen, Bernard, Philip Messing, and Robert Mlandinich. *Case Files of the NYPD: More than 175 Years of Solved and Unsolved Crimes*. Black Dog & Leventhal, 2018.
Benedetti, Matthew. "Cold Case: Why A Bomb That Killed Two Cops in 1940 Remains a Source of Intrigue." *NY City Lens*, March 13, 2020. https://nycitylens.com/cold-case-bomb-killed-two-cops-1940-remains-source-intrigue/.
"New York World's Fair 1939 and 1940 Incorporated Records." The New York Public Library Archives and Records, n.d. https://archives.nypl.org/mss/2233.

# About the Authors

**David Bushman** is the author of six nonfiction books, including two previous books on true crime: *Murder at Teal's Pond: Hazel Drew and the Mystery That Inspired Twin Peaks* and *Forget It, Jake, It's Schenectady: The True Story Behind 'The Place Beyond the Pines'*. He serves on the board of the New York chapter of the Mystery Writers of America. He spent over two decades as a television curator at The Paley Center for Media (formerly The Museum of Television + Radio) in New York. Before that he was program director at TV Land and a television editor at *Variety*.

**Mark Givens** co-authored the true crime Amazon bestseller *Murder at Teal's Pond: Hazel Drew and the Mystery That Inspired Twin Peaks*, published in January 2022 by Thomas & Mercer. His writing has been featured in the *Washington Post* and reviewed positively by *Vanity Fair*, *Publishers Weekly*, *Booklist*, and *Oxygen*. From 2015 to 2017 he hosted a Twin Peaks–centric podcast (www.deermeadowradio.com) that, after a long dormant state, is threatening to revive and regenerate itself any day now.

www.ingramcontent.com/pod-product-compliance
Lightning Source LLC
LaVergne TN
LVHW041636060526
838200LV00040B/1588